# Hydroponics Mastery:

### 3 books in 1
Hydroponics For Beginners + Hydroponics Garden + Hydroponics.

The guide to boost your gardening skills and build your own thriving home garden without anxiety.

By:
### Jamie Backyard

**JAMIE BACKYARD**

© **Copyright 2020 Jamie Backyard. All rights reserved.**

The content contained within this book may not be reproduced, duplicated or transmitted without direct written permission from the author or the publisher.

Under no circumstances will any blame or legal responsibility be held against the publisher, or author, for any damages, reparation, or monetary loss due to the information contained within this book. Either directly or indirectly.

**Legal Notice:**

This book is copyright protected. This book is only for personal use. You cannot amend, distribute, sell, use, quote or paraphrase any part, or the content within this book, without the consent of the author or publisher.

**Disclaimer Notice:**

Please note the information contained within this document is for educational and entertainment purposes only. All effort has been executed to present accurate, up to date, and reliable, complete information. No warranties of any kind are declared or implied. Readers acknowledge that the author is not engaging in the rendering of legal, financial, medical or professional advice. The content within this book has been derived from various sources. Please consult a licensed professional before attempting any techniques outlined in this book. By reading this document, the reader agrees that under no circumstances is the author responsible for any losses, direct or indirect, which are incurred as a result of the use of information contained within this document, including, but not limited to, — errors, omissions, or inaccuracies.

# THIS BOOK INCLUDES

## BOOK 1: 8 (FIRST PAGE)

### HYDROPONICS FOR BEGINNERS

A Starters' Guide For Learning The Basics Of Hydroponics And Set Up A Profitable System In Your Garden. How To Grow Fruits And Vegetables At Home All-Year-Round

## BOOK 2: 144 (FIRST PAGE)

### HYDROPONIC GARDEN

Discover How To Build An Inexpensive Garden At Home Even If You Are A Beginner. The Ultimate Diy Hydroponics System For Homegrown Organic Fruit, Herbs And Vegetables

## BOOK 3: 230 (FIRST PAGE)

### HYDROPONICS

A Step-By-Step Guide To Grow Plants In Your Greenhouse Garden. Discover The Secrets Of Hydroponics And Build An Inexpensive System At Home For Growing Herbs And Vegetables All-Year-Round

# Hydroponics for Beginners

A Starters' Guide for Learning the Basics of Hydroponics and Set Up a Profitable System in Your Garden. How to Grow Fruits and Vegetables at Home All-Year-Round

By:
## Jamie Backyard

**JAMIE BACKYARD**

# TABLE OF CONTENTS

Introduction..................................................................8

Chapter 1: Types Of Hydroponic Gardens.....................14

Chapter 2: The Correct Building For You ......................30

Chapter 3: How It Works ...............................................40

Chapter 4: Best Plants For Hydroponic Gardening And Nutrition ........................................................................64

Chapter 5: Hydroponic Garden Maintenance .................84

Chapter 6: Pest Control................................................104

Chapter 7: Myths And Mistakes To Avoid ....................124

Conclusion ..................................................................134

# Introduction

When we think of gardening, what we often see in our heads is a man or a woman on all fours crouched over a plot of dirt. They dig a hole, place in a seed or even a whole plant which they have bought, close it up and there you go. Or maybe we think of gardening in line with farming and we picture the same thing, only this time there isn't someone crouched down but a series of mechanical inventions that do all that busy work for them. We almost certainly don't think of an indoor setup, as that is more in line with hanging plants and decorative greens than it is with the concept of gardening. This would suggest that our main identifier which separates gardening from owning a few plants is the dirt itself, the soil which is part of Mother Earth. But the facts are quite different.

There are many different ways of gardening. The classic flowerbed in the front yard is just one of them. Here we'll be looking at another of them: Hydroponics. To say hydroponics is a new fad in the gardening world would discredit its history which reaches all the way back to the hanging gardens of Babylon and the Aztecs' floating gardens. There are even Egyptian hieroglyphs which describe a form of hydroponic. More recently, hydroponics was even given a place within NASA's space program. Clearly, this is not a new fad. But commercial growers and scientists are coming around to the method, leading to more hydroponic setups being used and more research looking into the advantages of hydroponics.

So, what makes hydroponic gardening different than traditional gardening? As the name implies (hydro) water plays a key role. The hydroponic garden actually doesn't make use of soil. Instead, hydroponic gardens make use of nutrient-based solutions through the circulation of water. So, a hydroponic garden tosses out the soil and instead uses an inert grow medium like clay pellets, vermiculite, perlite or one of several others that will pop up throughout this book. What this does is let the roots of the plant directly touch the nutrient solution, get more oxygen as they're not buried in the ground, and together these both promote growth.

The growth that this promotes can be quite astounding. A hydroponic setup, if managed properly, can actually see your plants maturing up to 25% faster than in typical soil gardening. Not only that but those plants that grow 25% faster might also yield up to 30% more as well! This is because the plants don't need to work as hard to get nutrients in a hydroponic setup as they would in a more traditional one.

Basically, with the roots getting everything they need to provide the plant with nutrients, the plant can focus on growing its top part rather than having to grow out its roots for sustenance.

But there are even more benefits to using a hydroponic setup than just expedient plant development. Despite the fact that hydro is in the name, hydroponic gardens actually use up less water than traditional soil-based gardens do. This is because the hydroponic system is an enclosed system. This means that there is less soil runoff, evaporation or wastewater in a hydroponic setup. Therefore, a hydroponic garden, when properly set up and maintained, will produce bigger plants at a faster rate with less environmental strain. It seems win-win-win, all around.

However, there are some slight disadvantages to hydroponic gardens over traditional soil-based gardens. The biggest and most obvious of these disadvantages is that a hydroponic garden will cost more to set up than a soil garden, regardless of size. With a soil garden, all you have to do is dig a hole, put in the plant or seed and then water it from time to time. This doesn't mean that you will have a healthy and well-functioning garden but it is pretty easy to get going. A hydroponic garden requires time and money to set up, especially if you've never set one up before. Plus, if you don't manage your hydroponic setup then it isn't very likely that it will keep those plants alive. Maintenance is super important here, that's why there's a whole chapter devoted to it later on. There are many different kinds of hydroponic gardens we can set up and some actually have more risks than others. For example, a setup that uses a pump (such as an ebb & flow system) can see that pump clog if not cared for properly and a clogged pump could see all your plants dead as result.

It should be noted that we are focused on hydroponic gardening which, despite the similarity in name, is not the same as aquaponic gardening. Aquaponic gardening is, in fact, a mixture of hydroponics with the growing and raising of fish. Basically, aquaponics is a hydroponic garden setup in which fish are introduced into the system. These fish create waste in the water which helps to give nutrients to the plants. The vegetables in the aquaponic garden, in return, clean the water for the fish. In this way, the aquaponic garden provides for both the fish that are being raised and the plants that are being grown. Aquaponic gardening is a great way of growing and raising food with an eye to sustainability. However, aquaponics gardening is beyond the scope of this specific book.

In this tome we will first explore the different types of hydroponic gardens we can set up. These will range from drip systems to ebb and flow systems, from aeroponics to wicking systems. We'll explore the advantages and disadvantages that they offer so that you have the knowledge you need to choose the type of system that works best for you. From there we will look into how these systems are built. While we won't be building every single kind of system that exists, we'll look at the general equipment that we need and explore the specifics of the most popular styles.

After we have our systems built, we'll talk about the operation cycle of hydroponic gardens. This means we'll explore how we set up our grow material, get seeds planted and discuss the different issues related to the lighting and trimming of our plants. Once we understand how to operate these systems, we'll take some time to examine the various plants that work best for hydroponic growth. We will also shed light on nutrition to figure out what exactly we mean when we use that word and what nutrients we feed into our systems.

With an understanding of the operation and nutrition of our hydroponic gardens, we will be able to move into a discussion on maintenance. This is one of the key areas that we need to grasp if we want to find success with our hydroponic gardens. Without proper maintenance, we can't expect to grow anything properly when we're fighting against clogs and bad pH levels. We'll move from maintenance into pests, which require another form of maintenance themselves. Thankfully, as we'll see, pests aren't nearly as common in a hydroponic setup as they are in traditional gardens. Finally, we will explore mistakes and myths that commonly pop up in regards to starting and maintaining a hydroponic garden.

While these gardens do take more time to set up than the traditional, the

knowledge in this book will give you a leg up in starting your own. But the benefits of hydroponic gardening speak for themselves: bigger plants in less time. Who wouldn't want that?

# Chapter 1:
# Types of Hydroponic Gardens

If we want to become hydroponic gardeners, the first thing we need to do is understand what options are available to us. This way we can choose a method that has advantages and disadvantages that are properly in line with what we are looking for. This means, for example, if we don't want to risk clogs, we could avoid using methods that involve pumps. However, if we live in an area where we have a hard time controlling the amount of light in our environment, we might find ourselves looking to a system that uses a pump rather than one of the simpler ones like a deep-water culture in which light regulation is also important.

Each of these systems offers unique advantages and disadvantages from which we can choose. But this does not mean that one particular system is better than another. Like most things in life, the choice of which hydroponic system to use should be based on your schedule, needs and abilities. For this reason, I won't be extolling the virtues of any one particular system. Instead, we will look at the most popular systems around to see what their benefits are and what their disadvantages are.

This way, you will have the knowledge necessary to choose the type that is right for you.

## Hydroponic system

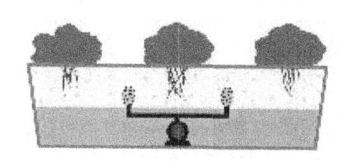

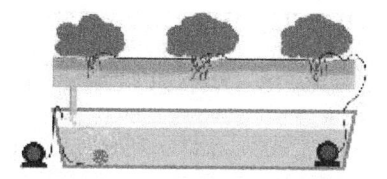

- Aeroponics
- Nutrient film technique
- Wick system
- Drip system

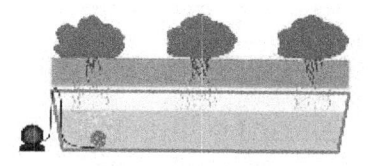

## Drip System

This system is one of the most popular hydroponic setups but it was actually invented for outdoor gardens in Israel. At its most simplified, the drip system uses a pump to keep a drip of nutrient-rich water feeding our plants. The slow drip, rather than the typical spraying of water we see in gardens, allows for less water to be used.

Typically, a drip system is designed with two key parts. The first is the reservoir of nutrient-rich water that will feed the plants. Above this rests the grow tray in which our plants are potted. A pump is set up in the water and is connected up into the grow tray. From there, each of the plants will be given their own drip line. This means if you are growing four plants in your tray, you would use four drip lines. Sixteen plants, sixteen drip lines. However, because we want to give the growing medium, that substance you use to replace soil (and which we'll be looking at more in chapter three), time to breathe so as not to drown the plants, these drips will use a timer system. The growing medium will slowly release the water back down into the reservoir, creating a closed system.

A drip system offers us great control over the amount of water and nutrients that our plants are getting. With this system we are able to control the drip both by quantity and by length. This means if we use too much water in our drip, we can dial it back; or, if our drip is going too long or too short, we can adjust the timers that we are using to experiment until we find the length that's just right. One of the cool things about the drip system is that while it may take a while to set up and get right in the early period, once we have everything in place and know our volumes, the system doesn't require as much overall maintenance (depending on the particular setup) as other methods will. Plus, the materials needed to create a drip system aren't as costly as some of the others.

However, a drip system still uses a pump and a clogged pump can see our gardens decimated in merely a few hours. Of course, this depends on the size of the system. While the drip system is great for large-scale grow operations, it might be too complex for smaller operations. Some drip systems use what is called a non-recovery system which means that the water is not circulated back into the reservoir. These particular systems require less maintenance than systems which do feedback into the reservoir but in doing so they create more waste. This means that regardless of the system we use, we either will require more maintenance or create more waste.

A drip system works well for a variety of herbs and plants ranging from lettuce, onions, and peas to radishes, cucumbers, strawberries and pumpkins. It turns out that these systems actually are fantastic for larger plants. They also work best when making use of a growing medium in which water drains slowly like peat moss or coconut coir.

So, if you are looking to grow larger plants, the drip system is a great choice. Drip systems do require a bit of maintenance and they can be slow to set up at first but once they get going, they offer a high level of control over the growing process that any gardener would love.

## Deep Water Culture

Considered the easiest of the hydroponic systems, a deep-water culture uses a reservoir system that the roots of the plants are suspended into. Basically, the plants sit above and instead of dripping water, they just reach down to take the water they want. This makes the system quite easy to set up. A deep-water culture gets its name from the use of a deep reservoir and from how deep the roots go into the water. Other systems, such as the nutrient film technique, expose the roots of the plants to the air so that they can absorb plenty of oxygen. With this system we set up a grow tray above our reservoir, making sure that the material we use stops light getting through the system to prevent algae from growing inside and messing up the system. From there, the roots are suspended in the water and the water itself is kept oxygenated through the use of an air pump. This is done to keep the roots from drowning in the water.

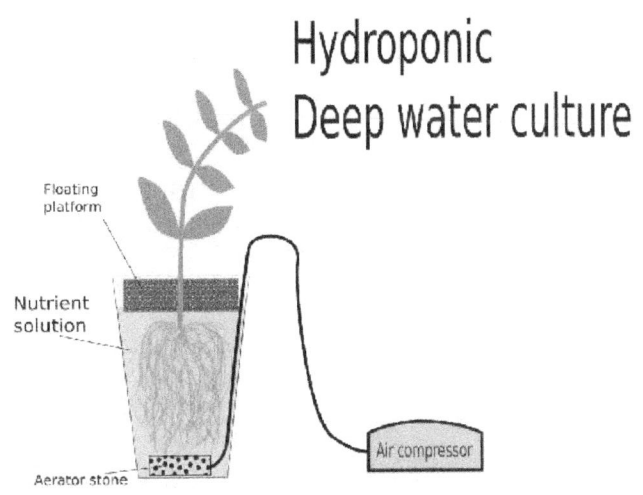

That's pretty much it. It wasn't a joke to say this is among the easiest of the hydroponic setups to get started with.

Deep water cultures are great for this simplicity but it is far from the only benefit that they offer. Because there are so few moving parts in a deep-water culture, they are rather low maintenance. There is an air pump but we don't pump water in this system and so the fear of losing our gardens to a faulty pump is unwarranted here. The easy setup and lower maintenance of these systems make them great for people first getting into hydroponic gardening and wanting to see if the approach is right for them.

However, while the deep-water culture's pump is air-based and so results in fewer blockages, they are still put at risk by power outages. Because the air pump is needed to oxygenate the water, a power outage could see your garden drown. Depending on the size of the system, it can be really tough to maintain proper pH levels in the water. A smaller system is harder to make minor changes in pH level to, as going just a little over or under can make a massive difference at smaller sizes. Finally, it can be really hard to keep a balanced water temperature in these systems as we have to be careful about the exposure of the reservoir to light.

Because of the way the system is set up, with the plants resting above the reservoir, the suitability of crops for the deep-water culture depends on several key factors. The first key is weight. If the plants we choose are too top-heavy, they can risk toppling over and breaking or even causing the weight of the setup to shift and knocking the top off. That's a disaster nobody wants to experience. The other major point is that we need to choose plants that like water. This means that plants which prefer dry growing conditions won't do very well in a deep-water culture. However, plants such as lettuce which love to soak up water will love this system.

Besides lettuce, some great choices for this system are herbs like basil and greens like kale, collard greens, chard and sorrel. Bok choy and okra also grow well in these systems and offer a variety outside of the traditional vegetables one thinks of as garden veggies.

So if you're looking to grow some water-loving plants, deep water culture is a system that is easy to set up and requires little maintenance. However, we have to be careful which plants we pick. If they are too top-heavy or prefer dry conditions, the deep-water reservoir isn't for them.

**Nutrient Film Technique**

With the nutrient film technique, we again use a reservoir of water but this time we are pumping it into a grow tray that has been set up at a slight angle. Doing it this way means that gravity takes care of getting the nutrient-rich water from one end of the tray to the other, where it will then drain back into the reservoir. More information about how we add nutrients to our water is covered in chapter four. Because of the design, this system is best used for plants with a smaller root system. The NFT setup is an active system.

The plants in the NFT system only have the ends of their roots touching the water, so as to keep the roots able to take in precious oxygen which helps growth. Because the system only uses a little water at a time, the plants are never drowned in the water.

Because of the way the plants are positioned, it is very easy to check the roots for disease in the NFT system. The use of a reservoir of water that feeds back into itself reduces the overall waste of water and the design of the system makes it easy to scale the project up or down depending on the size needed. Plus, unlike deep water cultures, it can be fairly easy to get the pH levels right using an NFT setup. However, the NFT also relies on a pump and so the risk of pump failure and the decimation of your crop is still a possibility that one has to look out for. Because of the way the roots are slotted into the system, they can block up the flow of water. This is why plants with a large root system like carrots aren't a good fit for the NFT system. Because the roots are not actually in a growing medium like the other systems we looked at, this means that top-heavy plants don't work here either. However, leafy greens like lettuce or fruits like strawberries have found great success growing through an NFT system.

## Ebb and Flow

The ebb and flow system get its name from the periodic flooding and draining of nutrient-rich water. It is also known, fittingly, as the flood and drain system. In this system, water floods into the glow tray and soaks the roots of the plants. Then the water drains back down into the reservoir. Flood, drain. Flood, drain. Over and over again, hence the name.

In order to get the system to work properly, we need to set up a pump to flood the grow tray. We set this pump up on a timer rather than let it constantly flood the grow tray and drown the plants. An overflow tube is set up in the grow tray so that the water drains back down into the reservoir. Depending on how we set it up, we might even include an air pump to make sure that the roots are getting the oxygen that they need.

The nice thing about the ebb and flow system is that it doesn't cost a lot to get started, as the materials aren't particularly hard to get a hold of. This system makes sure our plants are getting enough nutrients without drowning due to the easy to build structure. Once the system is set up, the hardest part of running it is out of the way. The ebb and flow system is able to run by itself once set up but you should still do maintenance to ensure everything is working properly.

Again, this system uses a pump, which means it can break and broken pumps are notorious for killing off entire gardens. If the structure fails to drain properly, the plants risk drowning and the pH levels in a broken system can be harmful to the plants. This is important to know because this system is prone to breakdowns and so we have to understand which areas a breakdown affects most.

One of the coolest things about the ebb and flow system is that it can be set up to allow just about any kind of plant or vegetable. Not so much the plants that prefer a dry system but size is not a concern here the way that it was in the nutrient film technique setup. Because of how easy it is to build the structure; we can alter it to fit the needs of our plants rather easily.

## Wicking

Out of all of the systems we have and will look at, wicking is the easiest. It is so easy, in fact, that it is often recommended as an entry point to hydroponic gardening.

Wicking is a passive system with very few parts, there are no water pumps in a wicked system.

In this system, we once again fill a reservoir with water and keep it beneath a grow tray. This time however, we don't use tubing to get the water to the plants but rather we set up a wicking material like rope. This wicking material is placed into the water and threaded up into the grow tray. Our grow tray is filled with a growing medium that is good at absorbing and keeping water because this system works very slowly. Water travels the length of the wick to slowly feed the plants.

This system is great for its simplicity and can serve as an easy way to start getting into hydroponic gardening. It is also an inexpensive system, making it that much easier for the novice grower to invest in. Because there is no pump to break down, this system isn't at risk for premature death the way pump-based systems are. The lack of a pump also means that this system doesn't use up electricity and it can be refreshing to those worried about the size of their power bill.

However, despite its simplicity, there are still downsides to the wicking system that we have to consider. The system is inefficient at delivering nutrients, so plants that need a lot of water and nutrients aren't a very good match.

The system can also see a toxic build-up of nutrients in the growing medium if we are not careful to observe how much water is getting in and being used.

Because of the lower water levels in wicking systems, they are best used for small plants. Lettuce and the smaller of the herbs make good fits for a wicking system but water-hungry plants like tomatoes would absolutely hate a wicking system. For this reason, the wicking system doesn't offer nearly the same variety as other systems. But that lack of variety is made up for by the ease of setup, making wicking a great system for those first trying their hands at hydroponics.

## Aeroponics

Saved the most complex for last. Aeroponics does away with the growing medium and instead leaves the roots of the plants exposed to more oxygen and so this system tends to see faster growth.

In this system, the roots of the plants hang down in the open air of the container in which the system is built. At the bottom of the system is our reservoir of nutrient-rich water. However, the roots don't dangle down into the water this time. Instead, we use a pump from the water to spray the plant roots with the nutrient solution. This pump is of course set up on a timer, to ensure we aren't overfeeding the plants. This makes it so that instead of the plant spending energy to grow out longer roots in search of nutrients, the nutrients come to the roots so that the plant can focus its growth elsewhere.

This system is great for producing larger plants since they don't need to focus on root growth. The lack of a growing medium also means that the roots don't need to take hold; we are bringing the nutrients directly onto them. The exposure of the roots to oxygen also helps to promote growth. This means that

the aeroponic system is known for producing crops with impressive yields. This system also doesn't require a lot of space can so it can be built to be fairly mobile. Because of the lack of a growing medium, the aeroponic system is rather easy to clean.

We have to make sure to clean it because the constantly wet atmosphere of the system makes for an environment in which bacteria and fungi can thrive. The system is also very much prone to failures related to pumps and loss of power, which we've seen can be a major killer of our hydroponic gardens. The setup of an aeroponic garden also costs more than the other systems and it is the most technical of the hydroponic systems, which means the knowledge to entry is much higher as well. They also require constant supervision to protect against root diseases, fungi and to monitor pH levels and the density of the nutrient solution.

However, this system allows for bigger yields and the system can be used to grow almost any kind of plant. This means that the variety the aeroponic system offers is unparalleled compared to the other systems we have looked at.

## Choosing the System That is Right for You

Like many things in life, the choice of which hydroponic system to use is a highly personal one

. Each of us is after different goals with our gardens and has different skill levels when it comes to handling the technical stuff. This means that the best option available to us in order to figure out which system to use is to ask questions based around our needs and desires, such as:

What is your skill level in putting together handy projects? If low, perhaps beginning with a wicking system would be an ideal start. What kinds of plants do you want to grow?

If you are looking for top-heavy and larger plants, you are going to need to use a system that can support them.

If you are looking for something smaller, you'll have more options but that doesn't mean you should go small if what you are after is a bigger plant.

Do you have the time to invest in one of the more maintenance-heavy setups or would a more streamlined one like wicking fit into your life and gardening goals better?

**BENEFITS OF HYDROPONICS**

**No Soil**
Lorem ipsum dolor sit amet, consectetur adipiscing elit, sed do eiusmod tempor.

**Water-Saving**
Lorem ipsum dolor sit amet, consectetur adipiscing elit, sed do eiusmod tempor.

**Fast Growth**
Lorem ipsum dolor sit amet, consectetur adipiscing elit, sed do eiusmod tempor.

**Higher Yields**
Lorem ipsum dolor sit amet, consectetur adipiscing elit, sed do eiusmod tempor.

**Less diseases**
Lorem ipsum dolor sit amet, consectetur adipiscing elit, sed do eiusmod tempor.

**Less pesticide use**
Lorem ipsum dolor sit amet, consectetur adipiscing elit, sed do eiusmod tempor.

**Affordable**
Lorem ipsum dolor sit amet, consectetur adipiscing elit, sed do eiusmod tempor.

Each of the setups that we have explored in this chapter has been written about and explored in depth throughout the internet with many first-hand accounts of how they turned out. If one strikes you as intriguing, there is always more research that can be done to make sure that it is right for you. But one thing that stands out when you research these is that each one has been used successfully and has been demonstrated to have grown some amazingly healthy- and good-looking plants.

You know what you desire more than anyone else. Looking at the benefits, the plant types and the cons should give you a good idea of where to start. I suggest narrowing down to the couple that interest you most and going from there.

In the next chapter, you will learn how to build your own hydroponic garden. We will look at how to set up a drip system, a wicking system and a deep-water culture. These range from beginner to intermediate in terms of difficulty setting up and so should make great entry points to those tackling hydroponic gardening for the first time.

# Chapter 2:
# The Correct Building For You

Now that we know the different kinds of hydroponic setups that are available to us, it is time to see how they are built. We will be looking at three of the different setups, those most suited for beginners. As we saw previously, each system has its own pros and cons.

This means that the system you choose should be the one that fits your desires. However, this chapter can also help you to determine which setup is right for you based on how difficult it is to get it running.

While there are many sites and businesses out there that will sell you hydroponic kits, it can be very easy to make them ourselves. This isn't to say there is no value in store-bought kits. But before we go spending a lot of money, a DIY setup can be a great way to get a handle on the basics of setting up a hydroponic garden. Once we know what we are doing, we can then start to add on all sorts of gears and gizmos to personalize and level up our gardens. But we have to start somewhere and DIY is a great place to kick off from.

## Drip System

For this system, we're going to look at one of the easy-to-build drip systems. This one uses buckets in which to grow the plants which still receive their nutrient-rich water through a series of tubes. In order to accomplish this design, there are three key areas which we need to build: the buckets, the reservoir and the tubing. We will look at what it takes to make a single plant setup but we'll see how easy it is to adapt the system to include more.

Start with your bucket. For our purposes, we'll begin with a five-gallon bucket but you can increase or decrease the size as necessary. The first thing we do is flip the bucket upside down so that we can get at the bottom easily. We're looking to get the drain into place so that any water dripped into the system will be recycled back into the reservoir. To do this we will be using a thru-hole fitting. These little guys are used in all sorts of different fields and you can easily pick one up for a dollar or two at any hardware store.

Place the thru hole on the bottom of the bucket, thread side making contact, and trace around it. This should give you a small little circle on the bottom of your buckets. We want this circle to be closer to the edge than to the middle, as we want our bucket to be able to sit comfortably on an elevated surface. With that in place, cut out the circle you have traced and insert the thru hole into the bucket. Tighten the thru hole in place. Your bucket now has a drain installed. Take a filter of some sort, can be a furnace filter or any kind really, and cut enough out to place over the thru hole inside the bucket. This helps to keep only water draining and not our growing medium.

Now before we move onto the next step, we should paint our buckets. We can double up this task and paint our reservoirs at the same time. Use a black paint on the outside of the bucket in order to block light from entering which would lead to algae growth. With the buckets painted black, they are going to attract a lot of heat which would raise the temperature of our water and could prove to be a real pain in the long run. For this reason, it is suggested that you use a coat or two of white paint over the black paint so as to reflect the light rather than absorb it.

We're going to do a similar design when it comes to our reservoir but the key difference is the hole we cut will be in the top and not in the bottom. Having painted the reservoir black and then white, we will cut a hole in the top of it through which we can feed the cording for our pump and for the hoses. That's all that the reservoir takes.

But in order to make this work from here, we need to connect them using tubing. Connect the tube to the hose and feed it up to the bucket. You can use glue, tape, or whatever method you prefer in order to keep the tube in place to feed your plants. One effective way is to create a loop that sits inside the inside of the bucket, poke a ton of little holes in it and then connect that tube to your main tube. That way water would flow up through the main tube, connect to the inner bucket tube and it would work like a mini sprinkler system. This way makes sure that the water is spread around the bucket and not confined to a single area.

With the feeder tube in place, we then need to attach the draining tube. This is as easy as hooking our tubing up to the thru hole we inserted and running it back down into the reservoir. It is important that we keep our grow bucket elevated above the reservoir so that gravity can do its trick.

In order to make sure that we aren't drowning our plants, it's important that we get a digital timer and hook it up so that we aren't pumping water at all times. We'll want to get a timer that allows us to set many different times rather than just one time because we want our system to turn off and on several times a day rather than just once. We need to do this in order to make sure that our plants are getting the right amount of nutrients.

So that is how you set up a single bucket drip system. If you want to expand the system, it is actually very easy. Let's say that you wanted to do four buckets instead of just one. You take those buckets and you give them their thru holes and a paint job all the same. The major difference between running a single bucket setup and a four bucket setup is the tubing. Rather than running a single tube from our reservoir to our bucket, we are going to instead use T-connectors. Take the tubing that runs out of the reservoir and connect it into a T- connector. This will give you a tube that looks like a T-corner like we see on the roads. Instead of being a single tube with one ending, you now have two tubes each with their own ending. This would allow us to use a two bucket setup. However, we choose a four bucket setup for this example. This means that we have to take each of those tubes and again run them into a T-connector. Now each side gets split into two and we have four ends, one for each of our buckets and we have quadrupled the size of our grow operation.

With all the building in place, we then just have to pack in our buckets. Some rocks at the bottom of each bucket can serve to help weigh them down but it's not absolutely needed. This is more a precaution, though it is one that is recommended. Over the rocks, you pack in your growing medium and then you get your plants in there.

And there you have it, your very own hydroponic drip system.

## Wicking System

As we saw above, wicking is actually the easiest of the systems to get started with. It's also one of the easiest systems to build as it requires very little technical skill. All we need to get started is a growing tray, a reservoir and a material for wicking.

Wicking is simply the use of a wickable material going from our reservoir to our grow tray. This can be rope, felt, string; whatever material you can easily get your hands on for the wicking will work.

We will first set up our reservoir, filling it with our nutrient solution of choice, which of course depends on what we are growing (for more information on nutrient solutions, see chapter four). Again, we are going to paint the reservoir black and then cover it in a coat of white paint to prevent it from supporting algae or growing too hot. We are then going to cut or drill very small holes in the cover of the reservoir through which we will thread our wicks.

Our grow trays are going to be filled with a medium that is particularly well- suited to wicking such as perlite or coco coir. But before we fill them up, we first want to cut or drill tiny holes into the bottom of the tray as we did to the cover of the reservoir. These will be roughly the same size because they are how the wick gets the nutrients to the plants.

Ultimately, we have our wicks almost entirely submerged in the water. This doesn't necessarily mean that they are touching the bottom of the reservoir but they are certainly coming close. They are then fed up and nested in the growing tray very close to the plants.

We can use more than one wick per plant depending on the plant's particular water and nutrient needs.

As far as set up, that's really it. We place our plants into the grow tray and we watch how they grow. However, there are some tips and tricks that will make a more successful wicking system. We might consider using an air pump to aerate the water so that our plants are able to get more oxygen as this will help them to grow faster. Another thing we will want to consider is keeping the grow tray closer to the reservoir with a wicking system than we would with a drip system. This is because the nutrients aren't pumped to our plants in this system but have to rely on what is called capillary action (aka, wicking). Having our wicks shorter means, they can more easily provide. The distance between our wicks and the grow tray is one way of doing this. Another is making sure that the level of the water in our reservoir is high, as this shortens the distance as well.

Again, this system isn't great for plants that require a lot of water and nutrients because the wicking of nutrients is a slow process. However, herbs and lettuce can grow great crops in a wicking system and this makes for an easy way to introduce the concepts of hydroponics to someone new to the topic. They even make great projects for getting kids into hydroponics and gardening!

## Deep Water Culture

Despite the wicking system being considered the easiest of the hydroponic systems to get started gardening with, the deep-water culture is just about as easy when it comes to building. For our purposes of explanation, we will be making a single deep-water culture. This means that we will be designing one as if we were growing a single medium-size plant. This system can be adapted to fit multiple smaller plants, though if we want to go bigger, we will have to change our culture to a larger container first.

Since a deep-water culture uses deep water (it's there in the name, after all), we will be using a five-gallon bucket because of the depth that it gives us. While some people refer to any system of plants floating on the water as a deep-water system, we actually need to have ten plus inches of water for it to be considered deep. We could grow a small plant in a small culture and have it be equivalent in ratios to that of a deep water culture but it still wouldn't be proper to call it such.

The first thing that we are going to do, surprise, is paint our bucket black and then white. Slightly underneath the lid, we are also going to cut a little hole for the tubing of our air pump so that we can oxygenate the water. With these two steps out of the way, we can set our buckets to the side.

Because a deep-water culture works by having the roots of the plant soaking in the water, we need to design a setup so that our plants can bath. To do this, we can go out and buy what is called a plant basket. This is a basket that looks like your typical plant pot but instead, it has a ton of holes through the lower half. Alternatively, we can also just take a plant pot and then cut, drill or solder holes into it. This is going to be our grow tray.

We'll be filling our grow tray up with our desired growing medium and the plant that we want to raise but first, we need to integrate it into the system. To do this we will be cutting a hole in the lid of our five-gallon bucket. At this point, it is best to cut a smaller hole and make it larger as needed rather than start with a large hole. This is because it is far easier to increase the size of the hole than it is to block it back up. If we make our hole too big, our grow tray will just fall into the bucket and we will need to get another lid and try all over again. Our goal is for the lower half of the pot to fit into the hole and be held in place by the pot's rim against the bucket's lid.

Earlier, we cut a hole in our bucket just under the lid for our air pump. The reason we didn't cut it on the lid itself is that when we open our system up to check the pH levels and make sure our nutrients are all balanced, we don't want to have to fiddle around with any wires. When we open our system, we should only have to remove the lid and thus the plant pot.

Everything should now be in place. We're going to fill up the bucket with our water, bringing it up to cover three-quarters of the plant pot that is hanging down inside it. We might want to test this first with plain water so that we can then mark the desired water level on our buckets to make it easier to see going forward. Mix together your nutrient solution, fill the plant potter with your desired growing medium and add your plant or seed.

It will take a week or so for the roots of the plant to start poking out of the holes that we drilled into our pot, so it is important to make sure that the water level is high enough for our plants to get the moisture they need. As the roots begin to hang down, the water level won't matter nearly as much.

And there you have it, you just created a deep-water culture for your plants. While you can grow a medium-sized plant or a couple of small ones in this one culture, you are most likely going to want to set up a couple. But as you've seen, that shouldn't take very much time at all.

In the next chapter, you will learn all about the operation cycle of hydroponic gardens. From the choice of growing medium to how we seed our plants and from lighting to trimming. While none of these steps are particularly difficult in and of themselves, we want to make sure that we have a strong grasp of each of them.

# Chapter 3:
# How It Works

Now that we have got a hydroponic system set up, let us take some time to look at how the operation works. This means that we will be exploring the different kinds of growing mediums available to us to see what works best for which kinds of setups.

We will also explore how we seed our hydroponic gardens, how we light them and what we do when the time comes for trimming.

**Growing Mediums**

When it comes to what medium we use in our grow trays, there is a ton of variety available to us. This can be a little intimidating at first when you aren't sure which medium is right for you and the gardening that you are looking to do.

It is important that we choose a medium that works with the plants we are planning to plant. This means that we have to take into account things like water retention and pH balance.

Before we look at the mediums themselves, a quick word on the requirements of the different systems.

The way that each system is set up and works actually says a lot about what kind of growing medium works best. For example, a drip system functions best when it is using a growing medium that doesn't become too soggy.

In contrast, a wick system likes a growing medium that absorbs and holds onto water and moisture with ease.

While nutrient film technique systems want to avoid a growing medium that easily saturates, an ebb and flow system will want to have good drainage and a growing medium that doesn't float. Considering the mechanics of your system of choice is the first step in deciding a growing medium.

**Coco Coir**

An organic and inert grow medium, coco coir is made from the frayed and ground husks of coconuts. When it comes to pH, coco coir is very close to neutral. Coco coir retains water but also allows a decent amount of oxygen to

get through which helps the roots. This medium is primarily used in container growing or in hydroponic systems of the passive variety such as wicking.

Because it can clog up pumps and drippers, it is not a great choice for more active systems such as the ebb and flow system.

## Gravel

Gravel doesn't absorb or retain moisture. Instead, gravel works to give an anchor for the roots of the plant. For this reason, gravel works best in a system which doesn't require a ton of retention such as a drip system or a nutrient film technique system. Any system that keeps the roots of the plant in constant contact with the water can make good use out of gravel.

In some setups, such as the bucket-based drip system we saw above, gravel is used as a bottom layer in the pot.

This allows for better drainage as the water has passed through whatever medium made up the top layer to find gravel which doesn't retain it whatsoever. It also serves to add some weight to the bottom of your tray which can help to prevent spills from wind or other elements.

If you are using gravel, make sure to give it a proper wash before use in the system. If you want to reuse the gravel, make sure to wash it yet again.

We do this to prevent salts or bacteria from getting into the hydroponic system and causing issues such as burnt roots, high levels of toxicity and the like. Jagged gravel can also damage the roots so it is best to use smooth gravel as a way of avoiding this.

**Perlite**

Perlite is actually an amendment to our growing mediums, which means that it is used to improve an existing medium rather than just being used on its own.

You make perlite by heating up glass or quartz sand, though of course we don't have to make it ourselves but can buy it from any gardening store. Perlite helps to improve the drainage and aeration when mixed in with another growing medium such as coco coir.

Because we are using a nutrient mix and not just pure water, we have to be concerned about nutrient build-up. The nutrients in our solutions can get absorbed into the grow medium and lead to a build-up of toxicity which risks killing off our plants No gardener wants that. The extra drainage that perlite offers will help to prevent this build-up and will help in making sure that our plant's root system get the oxygen it needs to grow. Perlite comes in different grades from fine and medium through to coarse. The kind you need will be determined by the rest of your potting mix. Perlite should never take up more than a third of your mix, however, as using too much will cause it to float and floating perlite doesn't offer the benefits, we wanted it for in the first place.

## Vermiculite

Vermiculite is actually a lot like perlite. It comes in three different grades, again ranging from fine and medium through to coarse. Made by expanding mica through heat, vermiculite is another soil and potting mix amendment. This means that vermiculite is mixed with another growing medium in order to get the best results.

Vermiculite sort of works like the reverse perlite. Where perlite helped with the drainage of our growing medium, vermiculite helps our growing medium to retain water. For this reason, vermiculite can often be seen mixed with perlite for use in hydroponic systems of the passive variety such as wicking systems.

**Rockwool**

One of the most popular of the growing mediums, Rockwool is made through the heating and spinning of certain silica-based rock into a cotton candy-like material. This creates a firm material that tends to have the ideal ratio of water to oxygen that our plants' roots love. It also is mostly pH neutral, which is always a plus.

It can be found in a bunch of different shapes and sizes with the most common being a cube shape. These cubes are awesome for starting out seeds (which we'll look at more in just a moment). These smaller cubes are often used in order to begin the growing of a plant before being transferred into another growing medium.

Because of the versatility of Rockwool, it can be used for starting plants before transferring into another medium for deep water cultures or nutrient film technique systems. It can also be used for drip systems and ebb and flow systems without the need to transfer.

## Mixing Your Growing Medium

When it comes to which growing medium is the best, it depends on the job that you are looking to have it tackle. Once you have an idea of what you need, you can begin the task of mixing it all together. There are many different projects on the market that offer pre-mixed growing mediums and these can be a great way to save a little time and get what you need right out of the box. However, some of us are a little more specific and we like to get our hands dirty in this part of the process. Mixing your own growing medium can be a great way to make sure it is 100% the way you want it to be. But this can be a little tricky if you are new to hydroponic gardening and don't know what combination of mediums is best. Part of getting into anything new, and hydroponic gardening is no different, is that you have to accept some uncomfortable moments and you have to accept that you will learn from your mistakes. For an example of one mixture, let us look at what Upstartfarmers.com have laid out in their discussion on soilless potting. They offer a formula for a mixture that is one-part coconut coir or peat, one-part perlite or vermiculture and two parts compost. While the systems we have looked at aren't focused on compost but rather getting nutrients through our reservoir's solution, this shows us a straightforward mixture. Notice that the perlite or vermiculite does not exceed 33% (or 1/3rd) of the total mixture.

## Seeding

When it comes to getting plants into our hydroponic system, we have two options available to us. We can go to the store and we can purchase a seedling which we then transplant into our system. Or we can purchase seeds and we can raise the plants ourselves. In this section, we will be looking at this second option to see how it is we can turn seeds into wonderful plants for our hydroponic gardens. But this means that we will also be exploring the first option because when our seeds are ready to be moved into our hydroponic setups, we will be transplanting them as seedlings.

There is a lot of satisfaction to be found in growing a plant out of a seed. They start out as tiny grains and yet can grow to be such big and luscious plants. It really is a wonderful feeling to know that you are the one responsible for making that come to pass. But there are benefits to growing from seed beyond just the feeling that it gives us.

When you purchase seeds, you are getting many chances at growing the plants you want. Not every seed will take but enough of them will that you can easily get a ton more plants through seeds for the same price that you would go out and get a single seedling. This makes it a cost-effective approach, as well as one that just feels really awesome. Purchasing seeds also gives you more control over what you grow, as you are not limited in options to only the seedlings that the store had available when you went looking. This means that you can be the one to choose what you grow and it could be rare and esoteric plants or just some lettuce and herbs. The choice is up to you.

If you grow the seeds directly in the hydroponic system which you are planning to use, then you don't have to worry about transplanting your greens into a new system. This can be a way to avoid causing the plants trauma or ending up with root damage. Transplanting into the system can also be a way to introduce disease or pests into your garden and we want to avoid this whenever possible.

When we decide that we are going to start with seeds, it does cost us a little bit of money upfront because we need to create a few things for them to start to grow. However, this cost is mostly when just beginning. If you have already started with seeds before, you can expect to save some money when you come to them next. The good news is that you really don't need to go out of your way to buy super specialized equipment or materials to begin growing from seeds. All of the materials that you pick up can have uses at other steps in the process.

Assuming that you have already gone and picked out some seeds, what do you need to get them started in your hydroponic garden? The first thing we need is a grow tray. This can be one that we have set up before, or we can make one with a dome shape to it so as to create a miniature greenhouse. Don't worry if you don't have one that fits that description, this is just one way to help our seeds out. We can use whatever grow tray we have available.

We want to make sure that we position our grow tray so that it gets good light - if the plants are the type that likes lots of light. We also want to make sure that the tray gets a good amount of heat. Getting a heating pad that goes under or making sure it is kept in a warm area will help to make sure that sprouting begins to happen.

At this stage, we have two options available to us. Our grow tray can be used specifically just for these seeds, which would mean that we have to transplant them when they have grown into seedlings, or we can use a grow tray that is ultimately part of the hydroponic setup itself. Going the second route can be useful because it avoids the traumas that can happen when trying to transplant our seedlings.

After we have a tray set up, we are going to want to go out and get or make some starting plugs. These are little compact masses of solid growing medium that are used specifically for the growing of our seeds They tend to be made up of composted pine and peat or other organic matter. We can purchase them or make them, as they are basically little cubes of the material with a small hole for us to put our seeds into.

Open up your plug and drop a couple of seeds inside of it. We do a couple just in case any of the seeds don't want to take. If multiple take, we can always remove the weaker plant so that the stronger one can grow even better. After you have dropped your seeds into the hole, tear off a tiny piece of the plug and use it to block the hole. You do this to prevent your seeds from drying out or getting knocked out of the plug.

In the grow tray, you will need about an inch of nutrient solution, though you only want that inch to be at half the strength that it would normally be at. Place the seeded plugs into the tray. You can expect to start seeing some sprouts emerge within four or five days from planting. Make sure that you keep an eye on the water levels throughout this period and add more nutrient solution as the levels decrease.

That's how you grow from seed. Now, if you have set this up in your main grow tray, you don't have to worry about transplanting them later and you can just let them grow and continue watching them as you would any other plant in your garden. If you started them in a tray specifically for seeds, however, then you are going to need to transplant them into your system.

As your seedlings start to grow stronger, you can stop worrying about halving the strength of the nutrient solution and begin them on the regular strength solution mix. When you start to see the roots of the seedlings coming out of the bottom of the starter plug, this is the sign that you can now begin transplanting them. This could be anywhere from two to four weeks; it all depends on which plants you are growing.

Now that the seedlings are ready, you are going to take them and gently move them over to your hydroponic setup. To do this you are going to take the seedling and the cube together. You want to open up a spot in your garden, gently place the cube and seedling into said spot and then cover it gently with your growing medium of choice. After this is done, you will want to water the plant from the top for a few days so that it grows out its root system and naturally seeks out water and nutrients.

And that's it! Now you have grown your very own plant from seed through to seedling and all the way through transplanting and developing a root system naturally. Working with seeds this way allows us to take more control over what we grow and to make sure that we aren't introducing any problems into our garden that may be found in the seedlings available for purchase at the store.

**Lighting**

When it comes to lighting, there can be no substitute that makes up for the power of the sun. There is a reason that spring and summer are such beautiful, green times of the year. The sun is absolutely the most powerful lighting source available for plants.

But we're not going to be using it here, despite all that. Instead, we are going to be using artificial lighting so that we have complete control over it. Not only that, but many of us are interested in hydroponics because we don't have access to an outdoor space in which to garden. If you live in an apartment, chances are you're reading this because it offers you an option for growing your own food without having to leave home. If you can set up your hydroponic garden so that it takes advantage of natural sunlight, that's great! But if you can't, you need to look into artificial lighting and that's what we'll be exploring.

There are tons upon tons of options available for lighting. So many that it can be really overwhelming if you are new to the topic. What size light do you want? What color spectrum is it supposed to be playing within? Heck, how much light is the right amount? It can truly be daunting. But don't worry, it's a lot easier than all those choices make it out to seem.

Tackling the amount of light, we can use the sun as a basis for this. If we were growing plants outside, we can expect them to need about five hours of direct sunlight and another ten of indirect sunlight. This means five hours soaking in the sun and ten hours being outside but getting a little shade. Using this system, we can adjust our artificial lighting accordingly. Using artificial lights, we should be giving our hydroponic garden about fourteen hours of bright light and ten hours of darkness. Doing this system everyday imitates the sun's natural lighting cycle. Don't skimp on the darkness, either. You might think that more light means faster growth but plants are just like us in that they need to rest and metabolize the nutrients that they are getting.

Some plants need more light, some plants need less. You can think of the fourteen-ten system as a general.

This system works well for most plants and can definitely be a successful route to take with your garden. But you should definitely be aware of the light requirements of your plants.

Some plants like short days, which means they want longer periods of darkness in which to function. With these plants, being exposed to more than twelve hours of light per day can actually cause them to not flower properly. Strawberries and cauliflower are examples of short-day plants. The short-day cycle actually works to imitate the shorter days of the spring in which these plants like to grow.

Long-day plants are those that want to get up to eighteen hours of sunlight per day. These ones are mimicking the longer day cycle that comes with the summer season. Examples of long-day plants include lettuce, potatoes, spinach and turnips. Because they like more light, you wouldn't want to mix long-day plants with short-day plants in the same growing tray. If you do, expect to pick a lighting cycle that meets in the middle of long and short needs.

There are also plants which are more neutral. These plants tend to be flexible and can work with more or less light as needed. Eggplant and corn are examples of these sorts of plants. Day-neutral plants can be mixed together with either short-day or long-day plants and grow equally well.

Because you want to mimic the sun, the best option for lighting your hydroponic garden is to get a timer. If you set up an ebb and flow system earlier, you probably have already gotten yourself a timer to make sure that you are letting your nutrient solution drain before washing over them again. We basically use the same kind of timer, only instead of being set up to a pump, we have set it up to our lights. How long you set the timer for will depend on what you are growing and their light needs as discussed above.

When it comes to the lights themselves, we need to get into a discussion on bulbs. The most popular bulb to use in hydroponics tends to be between 400- 600 watts and of a kind called High-Intensity Discharge.

These bulbs tend to be encased in glass (with gas and metal salts thrown into the mix) and they create light through sending electricity between two electrodes within. The gas helps the bulb to create the arc and the metal salts evaporate to make white light. They come in two types: high-pressure sodium bulbs and metal halide bulbs.

The metal halide bulb works as an all-round light that most vegetables will love. If you have to choose between metal halide or high-pressure sodium bulbs, the metal halide is the better choice. They tend to be expensive, upwards of
$150 for a 400-watt bulb but they only need to be replaced every other year, though they may decrease in efficiency earlier.

High-pressure sodium bulbs are best used for the flowering stage of our plants.

These are even more expensive than metal halide bulbs but they tend to last up to twice as long. However, they do also lose efficiency like the metal halide bulbs.

If we want to increase the efficiency of our bulbs, we can use a reflector hood.

This is a reflective case that goes around the bulb and increases its effectiveness by bouncing the light around. This helps the light to hit our plants from different angles so that we can get a more effective spread onto our garden.

It also serves to get a little more heat out of the bulbs, as the light beams are now crossing each other and make up a denser section and thus carry more heat and power.

So when it comes to lighting, if you can only get one bulb, go out and get yourself a metal halide bulb and a reflector hood.

Get yourself a timer and make sure that you set it to the needs of your plants. When buying plants, you almost always will receive a tag with some information about the light requirements of the plant or the seeds.

Following this and setting up an appropriate timer will make sure that your plants get all the light they need.

## Trimming

The final step in the operation cycle of our hydroponic gardens is trimming. When plants are out in the wild, nature plays the role of gardener and trimmer. These plants can go many years, sometimes even their whole life, without being trimmed or pruned. Once you bring your plants indoors, either inside with a hydroponic setup or in a greenhouse, people immediately start reaching for those pruning shears. When we consider the image of gardening we have in our heads, we can see that movies and TV have told us again and again that we want to prune our plants. Characters are always doing it!

But the truth is that if we don't prune our plants properly, we actually risk hurting them. To be clear, this means that the pruning we are doing is the thing that can hurt them. Not a lack of pruning. Improper pruning causes unneeded stress on our plants and can do some serious damage to them, even going so far as to leave them vulnerable to disease or infection. This is because each time we prune our plants, what we are doing is opening up a wound. We cut off a branch, we have just torn open our plants. Where there was a hand, figuratively, there is now just a stump. If you think about the human body, you can see why this could easily go wrong. We need to give our plants' bodies the same respect we would give another human's. This means that when you go to prune, make sure that you sterilize your cutting instrument between every cut.

This can be done as simply as mixing four parts water with one-part bleach and dunking your shears into the solution before each cut.

So if pruning our plants can be so harmful, what are the reasons that we choose to do it? There are actually quite a few reasons. One is that we want to control the overall size of our plants. If we are growing inside, we may prune our plants to prevent them from reaching out and getting in the way of walking areas or the television, things like that. This is the same reason that we cut tree branches when they get too close to power lines. We might also cut our plants to improve their health and the quality of their flowering. If a particular piece of the plant is dead and rotting, we need to remove that piece to promote the plant's health. We may also want to remove bits that didn't flower properly, that way the healthy flowering parts have more room to breathe and space to expand. This will also stop the plant from spending energy trying to repair damaged parts and instead it can use that energy for growing.

One reason NOT to trim your plants is to increase the overall yield. Trimming doesn't help our plants in this way. Rather than trim to increase, we should be trimming to promote better health.

When we have decided where we plan to prune, we know we need a sterilizing solution for our shears. Another way to prevent diseases during the pruning process is to pinch the ends of the plant where you have made the cut. This will help to get the ends to heal together quicker. It's kind of like stitching up a cut on your arm. You want to keep the ends together so that healing is promoted and the time it takes to heal is reduced. Because pruning the plant is so stressful and healing takes energy, you should really only prune when absolutely necessary and you shouldn't just make cuts willy nilly. It might be best to prune a little, wait for the plant to heal and then prune some more rather than do it all in one big burst.

If the reason you are pruning your plant is that it is growing too high for the area you are housing it in, consider doing what is called "topping." When we prune in this manner, what we are doing is cutting off the top of the main stem of the plant. Once we make the cut, we are going to then pinch it together as we do with any of our cuts. However, pinching the top of the main stem after a cut gets the plant to release floral hormones which will cause the plant to begin focusing on growing sideways rather than upwards. This same technique can then be applied to these lateral branches to achieve a reverse effect where it begins to grow upwards again. In this way, topping allows us to get some control over the growing patterns of our plants. Topping also leads to a weird effect where gardeners have noticed that plants which have been topped tend to produce more small fruit. Meanwhile, plants that haven't been topped tend to produce less fruit but of a large size.

If you are pruning to remove damaged and dying leaves, you should only be removing leaves that are more than half damaged. These leaves are no longer providing the plant with energy and instead are actually draining it of some in its attempts to heal them. There is a misguided idea that if a plant's leaves turn yellow, you should immediately remove them. However, turning leaves yellow is actually the plant's way of trying to tell you that something is wrong. It typically means that the plant is undergoing a lot of stress. This could mean that it isn't getting the nutrients and light it needs or maybe it is even a sign that the plant is dealing with an insect problem. When your plant's leaves start turning yellow, you should look at what the plant is trying to tell you before you start to cut it. If you fix the problem, quite often you will see the leaves take on their healthier green color again.

So, when it comes time to start pruning your plants, make sure that you sterilize your instruments, think about how much stress you are putting on the plant and only make cuts that are absolutely necessary. We want to grow healthy and fruitful plants and this means respecting the bodies of your plants like you would respect your own.

In the next chapter, you will learn all about the plants that work best in our hydroponic gardens. Not only that but we will take a look at the nutrients we are feeding them.

**JAMIE BACKYARD**

# Chapter 4:
# Best Plants For Hydroponic Gardening And Nutrition

We know what each of the hydroponic garden setups are, how we make several of our own and what kind of operation cycle we can expect to be going through. In this chapter, we are going to take a look at the different plants that are available for us to grow. We will take a brief look at each plant to get an idea of how they best grow in our hydroponic setups. From there we will be looking at the nutrition that our plants require.

## Vegetables

When it comes to vegetables, there are a ton of options available to us. We'll be looking at a handful of these but first, let's tackle some general rules of thumb.

First up are those vegetables that grow underneath the soil. These are vegetables like onions, carrots and potatoes. These plants can still be grown in a hydroponic system but they require extra work compared to those that grow above the surface like lettuce, cabbage and beans. This means that those under- the-soil plants require a little more advanced skill, and you may want to get some experience with your hydroponic system before you try to tackle them.

The other rule of thumb is that we should try to avoid crops like corn and zucchini and anything that relies on growing lots of vines. These types of plants take up a ton of space and just aren't very practical crops for hydroponic systems. Instead of focusing on a plant type that isn't practical, we can make better use of our space and systems.

**Beans**

There are many different types of beans from green beans to pole beans, lima beans to pinto beans. Depending on the type of bean you plant, you maywant to consider adding a trellis to your setup. Beans offer a wide variety for what you can add them to and they make a great side dish to just about any meal. When it comes to temperature, beans prefer a warm area. They also prefer a pH level of around 6.0. If you are growing your beans from seeds, you can expect them to take between three and eight days to germinate. From there you can expect another six to eight weeks before it is time to harvest. After harvesting begins, the crop can be continued for about another three or four months.

## Cucumbers

Like beans, there are a few different options when it comes to what kind of cucumber we can grow. There are thick-skinned American slicers, smooth- skinned Lebanese cucumbers, seedless European cucumbers. So a wide variety, and the best news is they all grow pretty well in a hydroponic setup. Where beans prefer a warm temperature, cucumbers prefer straight-up hot. They like to be a step beyond just warm. They also prefer a pH level between 5.5 and 6.0

It only takes between three and ten days for cucumbers to begin to germinate. They take between eight to ten weeks to get ready for harvesting. When it comes to harvesting cucumbers, make sure that the cucumbers have taken on a dark green color and that they are firm when you grasp them. Because each cucumber grows at a different rate, you can expect the harvesting to take some time as you don't want to pick them before they are ready.

**Kale**

Kale is a delicious and nutritious vegetable that makes a great addition to just about any meal. There are so many health benefits to kale that it is often considered a superfood. Kale actually prefers a slightly cooler temperature; it grows best in a range between cool to warm. Like cucumbers, kale prefers a 5.5 to 6.0 pH level.

Seed to germination only takes four to seven days. However, to get harvesting takes between nine and eleven weeks. It's a little bit longer to grow kale than either beans or cucumbers but you can harvest it in such a way so that it continues to grow. If you only harvest 30% of your kale when it comes time, this lets it quickly regrow. Doing this means that you can easily keep this superfood in your garden and in your diet.

## Lettuce

As you have been reading through this book, I would bet it's safe to say that no plant has popped up more often in our discussion than lettuce. This is because lettuce absolutely thrives in hydroponic growing conditions, which is great since lettuce can be used to make salads, give some texture and flavor to our sandwiches and burgers and is just an all-round versatile vegetable to have in the kitchen.

Growing lettuce offers a lot of variety. While lettuce prefers a cool temperature and a pH level between 6.0 and 7.0, it works in any of the hydroponic systems which you have made. For this reason, lettuce makes a great entry plant for getting into hydroponics. Lettuce only takes a couple of days to germinate but the time to harvest depends on what kind of lettuce you decided on growing. For example, loose-leaf lettuce only takes forty-five to fifty days to get to harvest. Romaine lettuce can take up to eighty-five days.

## Peppers

Like tomatoes, peppers are technically a fruit but are so tightly linked to vegetable-based dishes and crops that many people think of them as vegetables. For that reason, we'll be looking at both peppers and tomatoes in this section. Peppers share a lot of similarities to tomatoes in their growing preferences. Peppers like a pH level between 5.5 and 6.0 and a temperature in the range of warm to hot.

You can start peppers from seed or seedling. It takes about two to three months for your peppers to mature. When considering what kind of peppers to grow, know that jalapeno, habanero, mazurka, fellini, nairobi and cubico peppers all do fantastic in hydroponic growing.

## Radishes

Like lettuce, radishes are one of the easiest plants to grow, whether it be in a traditional soil garden or in a hydroponic setup. As suggested in the last chapter, radishes are best grown from a seed rather than seedling and it only takes between three to seven days to begin seeing seedlings from them. Radishes grow well in a setup with lettuce because both plants like cool temperatures and a pH level between 6.0 and 7.0.

What's really good about radishes is that they don't need any lights, unlike most plants. This means that if the cost of getting a light is too much for you right out the gate, radishes offer a way of trying out hydroponic gardening before dropping that cash. What's craziest of all is that radishes can grow super- fast, sometimes being ready to harvest within a month!

## Spinach

Another plant that grows well in combination with lettuce and radishes is spinach. Spinach enjoys cool temperatures and a pH level between 6.0 and 7.0, so it fits in perfectly. It needs a little lighter than radishes do but it doesn't require very much at all.

It'll take about seven to ten days to go from seed to seedling with spinach and can be ready to harvest within six weeks.

Harvesting can last up to twelve weeks depending on how you do. You can either harvest the spinach in full or you can pull off some leaves at a time. This makes spinach another great option for those first getting into hydroponic gardening.

**Tomatoes**

Okay, okay, we all know that tomatoes are technically a fruit. But we're looking at it here because together with the rest of the vegetables in this section, add tomatoes and you have one great salad! Tomatoes will grow best in a hot environment and you will want to set up a trellis in your grow tray. They also like a pH level between 5.5 and 6.5.

Tomatoes come in a variety; from the traditional ones we're looking at here through to those small cherry tomatoes that make delicious snacks. Germination can be expected between five to ten days and it will take a month or two before you begin to see fruit. You can expect it to take between fifty and a hundred days to be ready for harvesting and you will be able to tell by the size and color of the tomatoes.

**Fruits**

Nothing tastes sweeter than fruit that you have grown yourself. Hydroponic gardening offers a great way to grow some fruit inside the comfort of your own house. Like vegetables, there are many options available to us but we'll be focusing on those that grow the best.

<u>Blueberries</u>

Great for snacks, baking and even adding vitamins to your morning meal, blueberries are a fantastic crop to grow. However, blueberries can be quite difficult to germinate from seeds so it is recommended that you transplant blueberry plants instead. Blueberries are one of the slower plants to begin bearing fruit and can even take over a year to get to the point of producing. They like themselves a pH level between 4.5 and 6.0 in a warm climate.

## Strawberries

The most popular of all the fruits that we can grow hydroponically, you can find strawberries being grown in smaller personal hydroponic setups and in the larger commercial growing operations. Preferring a warm temperature and a pH level of 6.0, strawberries grow best in a nutrient film technique system.

Strawberries that are grown from seeds can take up to three years to mature to harvesting levels, meaning that, like blueberries, they are a long-term crop. Together, blueberries and strawberries make for great fruit crops which can produce for several years if you are able to give them the growing time they need.

## Herbs

Herbs make a great addition to any hydroponic setup. This is because it has been shown that herbs grown hydroponically have twenty to forty percent more aromatic oils than herbs that have been grown in a traditional soil garden. This means that you get more out of your hydroponic herbs with less used. This allows you to use less for the same end goal in your cooking, which means that your herbs will last you longer.

The best system for growing herbs is the ebb and flow system. Hydroponic herb gardens have been becoming a norm across the world because of their effectiveness. There are now even restaurants that grow their own hydroponic herb gardens on site because it is the most effective way to get fresh herbs of amazing quality.

Basil is the most popular of the herbs, with basil making up about 50% of the herb market in Europe. Both basil and mint like a warm environment and a pH level between 5.5 and 6.5. Similarly, chives prefer a warm to hot temperature and a pH sitting squarely around 6.0.

This means that if you are careful with the temperature and pH level you can grow all three of these wonderful herbs in the same hydroponic setup.

An herb garden is a great way to get started with hydroponics. They can stay harvestable for incredibly long periods of time; they taste better than herbs grown in soil and make great additions to just about any meal. Not only that but herb gardens tend to be smaller than vegetable or fruit gardens and so a hydroponic herb garden will take up less space and can save some money in setup costs.

**Hydroponic Nutrition**

In this section, we'll turn our attention towards the nutrient solution which we use to fill up our reservoirs and provide our plants with what they need to continue to grow and stay strong. In order to get an understanding of this important component of our hydroponic systems, we will explore macro and micronutrients, the importance of researching the needs of our plants and how we go about mixing our own solution so that pH levels and electrical conductivity are in proper ratios.

What is a Nutrient Solution?

When we talk about the nutrient solution we use in our reservoirs, we are speaking about a properly proportioned liquid fertilizer. While there are a ton of commercial options available on the market today, we will be exploring how we go about mixing our own.

This way, even if we decide to go with a store-bought option, we know how we can get the most control over our hydroponic garden's nutrition.

When it comes to growing plants, there are sixteen elements that combine together from the nutrients we use, our water and the oxygen in the air. A nutrient solution replaces those nutrients that would be found in the soil by combining them together into our water.

It is important to know what nutrients each of our plants want, as they are different from each other. There are more plants in this world than we can cover in one book, so it is important that you learn how to find this information for yourself.

The best way to do this is to open up Google and search "name of plant + nutrient requirements hydroponic". If you were growing tomatoes then this would look like "tomato nutrient requirements hydroponic". Looking at the search results you will find that almost all of them are titled something like "Tomato fertilizer requirements" or "Tomato crop nutrition" and "What nutrients do tomato plants need?" Each of these sites will offer you the information you need. I recommend that you look at several sites rather than just one, to see if the needs change or if a particular site offers more specific information.

## Primary Macronutrients

When we speak about primary macronutrients, we are referring to those nutrients that our plants require in large quantities. For humans, macronutrients are fat, protein and carbohydrates. While plants do care about these components, it is more for how they produce and handle them inside of themselves. When it comes to the nutrients they are after, our plants love nitrogen, phosphorus and potassium. We want to make sure that we have proper ratios of these big three so that our plants can stay at their healthiest, produce bigger yields and continue to grow.

## Nitrogen

Found in amino acids, chlorophyll and nucleic acids, nitrogen is an element made up of enzymes and proteins. While humans like protein in its pure form, plants like it when they get it through nitrogen. If your plants aren't getting enough nitrogen then they will have a lower protein content. Too much nitrogen, on the other hand, leads to darker leaves and it adds to vegetative plant augmentation. We want to make sure that our plants have a proper nitrogen balance because this will make sure that our plants are stronger, make better use of their own carbohydrates, stay healthier and manufacture more protein.

## Phosphorus

Phosphorus is actually a major element in the RNA, DNA and ATP system of our plants. This is a lot of scientific jargon to say that phosphorus is super important to our plants. A deficiency of phosphorus can cause our plants to take longer to mature. Not only that but the poor plant growth and root growth can also lead to a reduced yield and see the plant's fruits drop off before they are mature. Likewise, too much phosphorus can lead to a lack of zinc (a micronutrient) in our plants.

Our plants want to be getting enough phosphorus so that they can better make use of photosynthesis. It also helps our plants in controlling cell division and in regulating how they make use of starches and sugars.

## Potassium

The last of our three big macronutrients, potassium is slightly less important than nitrogen and phosphorus. This should not be taken as an excuse to ignore the potassium levels in our nutrient solutions. When our plants don't get enough potassium, they are at risk of having weaker stems and a reduced yield. Likewise, when we have too much potassium, we mess with the magnesium uptake of our plants.

When our plants are getting the right amount of potassium, we are making sure that they are using the water from our reservoirs to the best of their ability. Potassium also helps with our plants' resistance to disease, how they metabolize their nutrients and even how they regulate excess water.

## Micronutrients

When we speak about micronutrients, we are referring primarily to seven different nutrients that our plants like to have. These are boron, chlorine, copper, iron, manganese, molybdenum and zinc. Together these micronutrients aren't nearly as important as our macronutrients but are still very important.

Typically, horticulturalists only add micronutrients when their plants show signs of some sort of deficiency. However, before you start adding micronutrients into your mixture, you want to make sure that the issue is actually with the nutrients themselves. For example, a deficiency can be caused by pests or poor pH levels. If we go adding micronutrients into our mixtures when the problem had nothing to do with the micronutrients, then we are risking damaging our plants. For this reason, you should first consider all the possible causes and rule out as many as you can before you start reaching for micronutrients.

## Mixing Your Own Solution

The first thing we need to do when mixing our own solution is to figure out exactly what our plants need. We saw how we did this above in the section titled "What is a Nutrient Solution?" The information that you found in this section will let you know exactly what your plants want. We will take that information and use it here to fill out the specifics of this approach.

Before we get to mixing up our solution, we need to first go out and purchase some materials. We need to pick up some buckets. We need one bucket for each part of the solution. Three buckets tend to be a good number, as it allows us to tackle what they call an A, B, Bloom system. Some systems only require two buckets as there are only two steps to the mixture. You also want to buy a digital scale that can get down to hundredths of a gram. And of course, we need to purchase the nutrient salts that will be making up our solutions. These are salts which break down in water to give us the macronutrients we need. They can be bought at any hydroponic gardening store. Amazon.com also offers both premixed nutrient solutions and the raw nutrients you need to mix your own.

You will also want to make sure that you have some clean measuring cups and some rubber gloves to keep yourself safe. You want to fill the buckets up with the proper amount of water needed for each part of the solution. This will depend on what kind of mix your particular plants need and so will be a personalized amount. When it comes to our water, we need to make sure that it is clean. It is always better to use a filtration system to get rid of contaminants that may be present in the water.

You weigh out the proper amount of nutrient salt using the scale. Once you have this amount you pour the salt slowly into the first bucket of water. Do it slowly to stop it from splashing and losing some of the solution in the process. You should see the salts begin to dissolve almost as soon as they touch the water. After you finish the first one, measure out the salts for your second part of the solution. Repeat until all parts of the solution have been mixed in their own buckets. You may want to put lids on them and give them a shake to make sure that there are no clumps of nutrients left undissolved.

After we have our mixture (or mixtures) ready, we need to check the pH level. We know that most plants prefer something between 5.5 and 6.5. Water is a neutral medium which means that it has a pH level of 7. Get yourself some pH level testers and be prepared to get to work. We need to bring the level down a little bit. This means we have to adjust the pH level by mixing in a solution that is designed to lower the pH. These solutions are highly acidic, so you should only use a little bit at a time. You want to dilute the pH lower solution, so mix a couple of drops of it into a gallon of water. This should give you a solution closer to 2.0 or so. The nutrients you use raise the pH level of the water so you need to start from 2.0 and increase as you add the mixture. You then slowly add this diluted mixture into your nutrient solution. Make sure that you add this slowly and stop to check the pH level often.

After your pH level is in line, you will need to check the electrical conductivity of the mixture. To do this you need to get yourself an electronic EC meter. Electrical conductivity lets us get an accurate reading of the balance of nutrients and pH level. Since we have mixed our own nutrient solution, we have had to use mineral salts to get the nutrients we desire. We can figure out the number of nutrients in the solution through electrical conductivity. Most plants want an EC of somewhere between 1.5 and 2.5 so this can be a great way to check and make sure we've got a proper mixture before we feed it off to our plants.

If we come in lower than 1.5, this means we don't have enough nutrients in our solution and so we will need to add more in order to bring it up. Likewise, if it is too high then we risk subjecting our plants to nutrient burn. Nutrient burn refers to the physical signs that our plants are getting too many nutrients. Leaf scorch is an obvious sign of nutrient burn. Root burn is also another common symptom of nutrient burn. We want to raise healthy plants, so this means we shouldn't be overfeeding them too many nutrients.

Once you've checked to see that the EC level is where you want it, you have successfully mixed your own nutrient solution. While the specifics depend on the plants you choose to grow, this outline should show you that it really isn't that hard to prepare our own solutions and keep close control over our hydroponic systems and the health of our plants.

In the next chapter, you will learn all about how to keep your hydroponic garden in great working order through regular check-ups and maintenance. This includes sanitizing and sterilizing your equipment and trays. You'll see how we keep our reservoirs clean and clear of any problems. We'll look at root disease and how to handle salt build-up before it kills off your plants. You'll learn how to tell when algae becoming a problem and when to clean it out and you'll learn all about problems with fruiting and flowering.

# Chapter 5:
# Hydroponic Garden Maintenance

By this point, we have made our hydroponic systems, picked out the plants we want to grow and mixed together a batch of nutrient solution to give them all the macronutrients they could ever desire. By now, it is safe to call yourself a hydroponic gardener! But the work hasn't finished yet. Now that you have your setup and you are growing your plants; you have to remain vigilant in maintaining your hydroponic garden.

This chapter is packed full of tools to help make sure that your garden continues to run smoothly. To this end, we'll look at how we sanitize our growing space, as well as how we go about sterilizing it. These two words are often used interchangeably but are actually two different steps. From there we will explore the ways we can keep our reservoirs in good condition, look at some general troubleshooting advice and speak on how our plants tell us that they need help. Because of how super important the information in this section is, we will close out the sections with a quick recap on the actions you should be taking for your garden.

## Sanitizing

When it comes to sanitizing our hydroponic gardens, what we mean is that we are giving our garden a deep clean. It is as important to keep our gardens clean as changing a burnt-out lightbulb is or making sure that our nutrient solution is properly balanced. A proper sanitization will kill off and get rid of most microorganisms that can cause damage. Sanitizing doesn't mean that you are using a cleaning product or a chemical solution. While this can be a part of sanitizing, sanitizing can be as simple as a wipe down and the removal of any filth and dead plant matter.

The first step in sanitizing which you will want to take is to make sure that any spills, excess water or plant runoff is immediately cleaned up. You can purchase a wet/dry vacuum which can help in cleaning up spills but, while this is a useful tool, you can do this cleaning by hand as well. You want to make sure that you are getting these spills quickly and cleaning them up fully because the extra moisture on the floor can raise the room's humidity. A rise in humidity increases the risk that mold will take up residence in our systems. It also risks exposing our plants to rot, which is a plant's worst nightmare. Not only that, but spills can actually damage your floors which can lead to having to pay for repairs.

Any time you enter into the room in which you keep your hydroponic garden, you want to keep an eye out for any dead plant matter that you can find. You should take the time every day to check for fallen leaves and other dead plant matter. While it is easy to just check your grow tray and call it a day, make sure you check the floor around your garden as plant matter can easily escape and out of sight doesn't mean it isn't hurting your plants. These will fall into your grow tray or onto the floor around your garden. We want to clean up this dead plant matter because it is extremely enticing to mold and fungi. It is also extremely enticing to a variety of pests (we'll see how to deal with those in the next chapter). Make sure when you harvest your crops that you always get rid of old root and plant matter rather than leave it for later.

When it comes to facing problems with plant rot, a lot of gardeners never realize that the problem stems from the cleanliness of the grow room. In the last chapter, we saw that we want to make sure that the problem with our plants is not something else before we start adding micronutrients into our solutions.

This is one of those situations where people jump to conclusions. However, one of the first things we should be checking is that we have kept a clean garden space.

If your hydroponic setup uses an intake filter, then you are going to want to inspect and clean that filter at least once a week or so.

These filters help to keep dust, bugs and molds from getting into our growing trays. Routine cleaning of the intake filter will make sure that your system keeps maximum airflow. It will also be a way to get an early warning of any pests that are trying to get into your garden. Finding a pest on the intake filter gives you a head start on preventing them from messing up and damaging your garden.

Once every few months or so you should also take out the bulbs from your lights and give them a wipe. You should also do this with any glass you have such as when you use a reflector with your lights. Setting a schedule to do this, say, every three months, will allow you to plan it out ahead of time and to make sure that you don't neglect this cleaning. Harvesting can also be a great time to get at this cleaning, as when we harvest our plants, we tend to open up more space and make it easier to get at our equipment. Glass cleaners or isopropyl alcohol can be used to clean this glass. We want to keep up with this cleaning as grime can build up on our glass and lights and this can reduce the light output that we are able to give our plants.

You will also want to sanitize the hardware in your grow room about as often as you clean the glass. This means wiping down our pumps, hoses, all the stuff like that. You'll even want to wipe down the outside of your grow tray and your reservoir. If you have equipment that has exposed circuitry then you will want to get a couple of cans of compressed air so that you can clean these without damaging any of the electronics.

To recap: Clean up any spills as soon as they happen. Check for dead plant material once a day. Check your intake filters on a weekly basis. Every couple of months you should get in and clean the glass and bulbs used in your lighting setup. Around the time you clean your glass, you should also give any hardware you are using a quick clean, using compressed air on anything with exposed circuitry.

## Sterilization

When it comes to cleaning, sterilization is a more involved process than sanitization is. We sterilize our equipment in order to kill off microorganisms like bacteria, spores and fungi.

Because we are speaking on hydroponic systems with the assumption that they will be kept indoors, we will look at how we use chemical cleaners to sterilize our equipment. We can also use heat and filtration but these are more involved and complicated and are more useful for large-scale growing operations.

Unlike sanitization, we don't want to sterilize nearly as often. With sanitization, some of the practices are best used on a daily or a weekly basis.

Sterilization should be used far less often because not only is it unnecessary but it can also hurt our system and our plants. For one, it takes more time and thought to sterilize and it can leave nasty by-products if we aren't careful to rinse properly afterward. When it comes to sterilization, we will be primarily looking at sterilizing our trays and reservoir, as well as the inside of any tubes we must clean.

The two most common chemical cleaners for sterilization are bleach and hydrogen peroxide. Bleach typically contains sodium hypochlorite as its active ingredient. This is the same chemical which is used to disinfect wastewater. While bleach makes for a great sterilizer, it can leave residual traces on our equipment and so if you choose to use bleach you should be prepared to double and triple rinse anything you cleaned using it. After you harvest your plants but before you set up the next batch to grow is a great time for a bleach bath. Using a mixture of one-part bleach to one part water, you should soak any air stones or other submersibles as well as your tray and reservoir. Make sure that you rinse these off two or three times, just to be extra sure that no harmful residue is left.

Hydrogen peroxide is actually just water that has an unstable oxygen molecule. This makes it a great chemical cleaner as instead of leaving behind a harmful residue it actually breaks down into water. Since water doesn't hurt our plants, using hydrogen peroxide means you don't have to worry as much about the double or triple rinsing that bleach requires. You can use a rag that has been soaked in 3% hydrogen peroxide to wipe down and clean your components. If you have a larger setup, you may consider creating a hydrogen peroxide solution that you can have run through the system. For this, you would want to keep it at about 35% hydrogen peroxide. If you run a hydrogen peroxide mix through your system, make sure that you send some water through to rinse afterward before you return your plants to the system.

To recap: You shouldn't sterilize too often as this can hurt your plants. A good time to sterilize is between harvesting and setting up the new crop. If you use bleach to sterilize, make sure you double or triple rinse afterward to prevent residue from hurting your plants.

## Maintaining Your Reservoir

When it comes to our gardens, it is clear that we have a favorite section. All the greenery at the top is just so pretty and exciting to watch grow. It can be easy to maintain a habit of removing the dead leaves that have fallen because it is fun to poke around our plants and see how they are doing. But while it is easy to focus up top, we can't let ourselves forget about how important the bottom of our system is too. Without the reservoir of nutrient solution, our plants wouldn't get what they need to grow and we would just have one dead garden.

Our reservoirs are such an important part of our hydroponic systems that we should make it our mission to see that they are kept in the best possible shape. To do that, there are several steps and behaviors that we should adapt to make sure we stay on top of reservoir maintenance.

The first step we should take is making sure that our reservoirs are kept at a proper temperature. If we let our reservoirs get too hot then the levels of oxygen go down and create conditions for root rot to flourish. We want to keep our nutrient solution around 65-75 degrees. If our reservoirs are too cold, we can always get an aquarium heater or a heating pad to raise the temperature up. If our reservoirs are too hot then there are several options available to us. We can get a reservoir chiller, move our setups into the shade, or add some ice cubes to our solution. We also want to make sure that after we paint our reservoir black, we then add a coat of white paint to help reflect rather than absorb heat.

If your hydroponic garden is using a circulating system, then you are going to need to make sure that you check on your water levels and top up the reservoir. We lose water to evaporation and to processes that our plants undergo. This means that water loss is a part of the gardening experience and so we should be prepared to top up what is lost. This is especially important with smaller systems, as the loss of a little bit of water in a smaller system is a bigger deal.

Once every week or every other week you should consider changing out the water in your reservoir. This is a process that can get very specific for each garden. Knowing when it is time to change is something that you will grow into. But to start, assume every two weeks. Using your EC meter can help you to know when the time is right. While the EC reader will let us know how much

fertilizer is in our solutions, it doesn't give us a breakdown of how much of each nutrient is left. Our plants don't use every nutrient the same way, some are absorbed and processed quicker than others. This means that even when we are checking levels with our EC meter and seeing that there are enough nutrients, we can actually have too much of one kind and not enough of another. When we change out our water, we are able to make sure that we provide our plants with a freshly balanced nutrient solution. It also gives us a chance to sanitize our reservoirs.

Speaking of our EC meters, we want to make sure we are doing regular EC checks. Of course, the numbers we are aiming for here depend on what plants we are growing. By this point, you should already have researched proper EC levels for your plant of choice. You also want to make sure to do regular pH level checks. We know that we want to keep our pH around roughly 5.5 to 6.5.

Finally, the most important step of all is to make sure you are checking your pumps regularly. You want to get on top of any build-ups that may be growing in your pumps. We want to do this because nothing kills off a garden faster than a broken pump. Making sure to clean out your pumps and clear away any nutrient build-ups will go a long way to keeping your garden healthy and keeping your reservoir working as intended.

To recap: Keep your reservoir between 65-75 degrees. Check the water levels and top them up often. Change the water out of your reservoir every other week. Use an EC meter and pH tests to keep your levels in check. Check your pumps regularly to prevent blockages.

**Salt Build-up and Salt Burn**

Have you ever seen a garden that has a white (or off-white) build-up of crystalline crust on the stems of the plants or the top of the growing medium? This is what is called a salt build-up and it is very bad for your plants. A salt build-up can lead to salt burn. Salt burn around the roots will lead to the stem at the base of the plant dying. This leads to wilting during the hotter moments of the day and it can even open this area of your plant up as the perfect feasting ground for disease.

Salt build-up happens when your growing medium loses moisture to evaporation at a faster rate than the plants are able to use up the nutrients. The moisture evaporates but the nutrients stay behind and jack up the EC levels in the medium. The good news is that salt build-up is easy to handle as long as you know that's what you're dealing with.

That white crust on the stems and top of your growing medium is a dead giveaway. If you are seeing that white crust and you notice that your plants have become stunted in their growth, have taken on a darker color or are growing uncharacteristically slow, then you should have all the signs you need to diagnose a salt build-up. One way you can confirm your suspicions is to take an EC reading of the solution that drains from your growing tray. If the EC reading increases on draining, you almost certainly have a salt build-up problem.

If you have identified a salt build-up as a problem in your garden, then you are going to want to flush your growing media. While some gardeners will flush their system with plain water, this can actually have a negative effect. If there is a crop already growing, the drop in osmotic pressure can cause the plants to take in a ton of moisture around the roots. This can lead to fruit splitting or the vegetative growth coming in soft and weak.

A healthier approach to flushing the growing medium is to use a flushing solution that has been premixed, such as you can find at any hydroponic store.

You can also flush with a nutrient solution that is at one third the regular strength. Depending on your setup, you may find yourself needing to do this flush every few weeks such as if you have an ebb and flow system in a warm climate where evaporation happens easily.

To recap: You can identify salt build-up by a white crust on the top of your grow medium and on the bottom of your plant stems. This happens because of evaporation that leaves the nutrients stuck there. Use a nutrient solution flush at one-third of regular strength in order to clear away the build-up.

**Algae**

If you are running a hydroponic garden, you will have to deal with algae at some point, I promise. Therefore, it is important that you know what to keep a lookout for.

Algae will look like a slimy growth that clings onto the different parts of your setup. It can be brown, green, reddish or black. You shouldn't be surprised if you find long strings of algae in your system and you shouldn't be surprised if it seems like it just showed up out of nowhere. Algae can grow super-fast.

Algae also smells horrible. It has a moldy, earthy scent to it. When you get a ton of algae decomposing in your system, it will give off an unpleasant odor that can be a sign that you have a serious algae build-up on your hands.

Algae can be a real pain. First off, it is really quite disgusting looking. But far worse than its esthetical value and its smell is the fact that algae can easily block up your drippers, pumps and any other component of your hydroponic system that is prone to blockages.

Like we saw, this can easily kill off your garden. Not only that but if you have a serious algae problem it can even block off your growing substrates and steal oxygen away from your plants. When this starts to happen, it can lead to an increase in the biological oxygen demand of your system. This means that your plants won't be getting enough oxygen and this can lead to their roots suffocating. If algae attach directly to your plants' roots, then it can leave your plants at risk for pathogens like Pythium.

Algae itself can really suck but it gets even worse when it begins to break down and decompose. When this happens, it can actually release toxins into your system. These toxins then act as a food source for pathogenic fungi. When this begins to happen fungi can seem to just suddenly pop up and get a strong foothold in your system.

Most hydroponic growers tolerate a small number of algae in their systems because it can be difficult to get rid of. If you are taking care of your reservoir and making sure to clean it, then you can also take care of algae at this point. Make sure that you scrub down your systems between grows so that any algae that has gotten a foothold is removed. Some growers will use algaecide products in their nutrient solution to kill off algae but this can also cause our plants to be damaged. Not only that but algae regrow quite quickly after the use of algaecide products. This means that you will have to add in more algaecide soon afterward, thus risking your plants' health yet again.

To recap: A little bit of algae is fine but a major problem needs to be handled before it decomposes or it blocks up pumps and working components of your system. Clean by hand rather than using algaecides.

## Maintaining Root Health

When it comes to the health of our roots, the most common killers are starvation, suffocation, damage from chemicals, pathogens, temperature or the EC/pH levels. The leading cause of root death and poor growing rates is suffocation. Many pathogens won't attack a healthy root system until they have been damaged due to poor conditions. Suffocation happens when there is a lack of oxygen getting to the plants such as when there is too much decomposing organic matter in our reservoirs, slow flow rates or too many plants all fighting to get enough oxygen.

As the roots begin to suffocate due to lack of oxygen, toxins will start to proliferate. Some plants will try to grow new roots to find alternative sources of oxygen but many will just up and die. If your plants aren't getting enough oxygen, consider adding an oxygen stone to your reservoir.

If there aren't enough nutrients moving through your system, this will have an effect on the root system the same way that it affects the top part of the plant. However, it can be harder to tell that there is an issue with the roots. A lack of phosphate will cause the roots to turn brown and you will see a reduction in the number of lateral branches. A calcium deficiency causes the root system to thin out and develop a sickly brown color. Lack of manganese will lead to a root system that is shorter and finer than normal and you'll notice the tips of the roots browning. These each are clues that you want to take care of your nutrient solution and reservoir.

Another thing can lead to damaging our plants' roots are improperly balanced EC and pH levels. An unbalanced system will lead to severe stunting of the roots. At higher EC levels water will be lost from the roots and lead to root death. This is a common response from plants that enjoy a lower EC level. When pH levels get to be too high or too low then we can see root damage and problems with nutrient uptake. However, plants will take much kindlier to fluctuations in pH levels than they will in EC levels.

When it comes to root diseases, setups that use a recirculating system for the nutrient solution present the most risk. This is because the circulating of the solution can easily carry pathogens through to all of our plants. Some pathogens will attack the roots in a hydroponic system in a way that makes them easy to identify while others will seem almost invisible. Regardless if they show or not, all pathogens will lead to a reduction in the growth of your plants and the amount they yield. The most common pathogens that mess with our roots are didymella, verticillium, olpidium, plasmopara, pythium, fusarium and phytophthora.

Pathogens that affect your roots can come from a variety of sources. They can be airborne, waterborne, found in your growing medium, arrive from insects and pests, infected plant matter or even from seeds and dust. While airborne pathogens that damage your roots are rare, they can still happen. One of the most common sources for infection comes from soil. Soil can get into a hydroponic system from your hands, shoes, dust in the air, from our equipment or even from the water we use in our reservoir.

Root diseases and the pathogens that cause them like to attack plants that are already undergoing a lot of stress. Because stressed plants leave your system open to attack, the best way to defend against these pathogens is to make sure that your crop is healthy and not undergoing undue stress such as when we trim stems too often. Another cause of stress is our roots not getting enough oxygen, such as when algae has grown into a major problem.

One of the best behaviors we can get into is making sure that we take the time to check on the root system of our plants. Most of us want to poke around on the top part where it's all green and pretty.

While it is important that we take care of our tops, we must not forget the bottom. Checking the roots on a regular basis will be a great tool for catching a problem before it becomes a crisis.

If your plant is wilting or looks discolored then you should make sure to check the root system.

If you identify that a plant has or potentially has root disease, then your first step should be to remove it from the garden and destroy it. If a plant is diseased and you leave it in the system, you risk that disease being carried to the other healthy plants. These pathogens can survive and go from one crop to the next, so it is important that you sanitize and sterilize your hydroponic system between crops.

To recap: Root health is just as important as the health of our tops. A lack of oxygen is the most common problem for our roots. Avoid stressing the plants by doing regular checks of the EC and pH levels. Identify issues with roots so that you can remove diseased plants before they spread to healthy plants.

**Fruiting and Flowering**

When it comes to problems with our crops fruiting and flowering there can be a lot of different causes. These range from a lack of fruit development through to physiological disorders such as blossom end rot. You may find your fruits have skin disorders like blotches, streaks, silvering or uneven color. Another issue is fruit splitting which leads to ugly looking plants that are horribly misshapen.

Many hydroponic crops will begin to flower and fruit when they reach a proper age. If there is a problem with the fruiting, you may run into a problem with flower dropping. This is when the flowers and fruits drop off the plant

before they are ready. This can be caused by external problems but it can also be internal such as when our plants are undergoing an undue amount of stress. A lot of crops will run into flower drop if the air temperatures are too high. The point at which heat affects plants is different for each kind. If your plants aren't getting enough light, this can also lead to flower drop. A lack of light also can stunt the growth of the whole plant.

Flower drop can also be caused by nutrient deficiencies. Common causes of flower drop due to deficiency are when our plants aren't getting enough nitrogen or phosphorus from the nutrient solution we have made. Stress caused by water can also lead to flower drop. This is stress caused by a poor irrigation system or from having an EC level that is too high. For this reason, we want to make sure that we are checking the EC levels of our nutrient solutions on a regular basis.

Another cause of fruit drop is when the weight of the fruit is too heavy for the plant to hold onto. This can be due to the weight of the fruit or the weight of the vegetative growth itself. For this reason, we want to make sure that we are trimming our plants in a healthy manner that promotes a manageable growth such as when we top our plants. When there are larger fruits growing on our plants, this can lead to the dropping of smaller fruits. This can actually serve to help the healthier, larger fruits to continue growing. Likewise, we may consider removing smaller fruits so that the energy spent growing them is redirected.

To recap: Issues with flowering and fruiting tend to be related to stress. Make sure to take good care of your plants, remove unhealthy fruits and give heavy plants support to prevent dropping.

In the next chapter, you will learn all about the different kinds of pests that can try to take up a foothold in your garden. Along with a look at the pests themselves, you will learn how we take care of them so that we can keep our hydroponic gardens in the best shape possible.

# Chapter 6:
# Pest Control

We've made it through setting up our own hydroponic garden, picking plants, learning about nutrients and figuring out how we can maintain it. But now we've come across a whole new issue: Pests. Our setup provided a great environment for our plants to grow. But it also created an environment which pests love and we even filled it with tons of healthy plants for them to eat. This would be fine if they provided some kind of service to our plants but all they want to do is snack on them and leave them wilted and yellowed.

In this chapter, we'll take a look at the most common pests that hydroponic growers encounter and we'll see how you can spot them in your own garden. Our number one defense against pests is to prevent them from making our gardens their home in the first place, so we will learn some of the techniques used to detect them early and prevent an infestation.

Pests aren't the only problem we face as hydroponic growers. Disease is also something we must be vigilant in spotting, identifying and handling.

To this end, we'll look at some of the more common diseases and how we can prevent them. A lot of this information was covered in chapter five, so we will be referring to it often here.

## Common Hydroponic Pests

While there are many pests that can try to make our gardens their home, there are certain pests that show up with more regularity than others.

These pests fall into five key categories: spider mites, thrips, fungus gnats, whiteflies and aphids. If you find yourself with an infestation of pests, it is a safe bet that they'll fall into one of these five categories.

## Spider Mites

Out of all five types of pest, spider mites are a particularly annoying one. While they are less than a millimeter long, these little guys are actually tiny spiders.

Because they are so small, they have a tendency to start damaging your plants before you even notice that they have taken up in your garden. Spider mite damage will look like tiny brown and yellow spots on the leaves of your plants.

While they don't look like anything serious when there are only a couple of bites, this damage adds up quickly to really wreak havoc on your garden.

To spot a spider mite infestation, there are two key signs to look out for. While the damage on your plants can be a telltale sign, it doesn't specifically tell you that spider mites are the problem. To spot a spider mite infestation you should check your plants to see if you can spot any spider-like webbing. Another way to check for spider mites is to use a tissue or clean rag to gently wipe the bottoms of your leaves. If you come away with streaks of blood, this will tell you that you have a spider mite problem.

One way of handling spider mites is to wash your plants down with a hose or powerful spray bottle. The force of the water can often knock the mites off of your plant and drown them in the growing medium. Spider mites also have some natural enemies ranging from ladybugs to lacewings and you may consider adding these beneficial insects to your garden to feed on the spider mite population.

## Aphids

These little guys are also known as plant lice. And just like head lice, they aren't all that much fun. These tiny, soft-bodied pests are pretty much able to set up in any environment. They multiply quicker than rabbits, so you want to make sure to tackle an aphid infestation as soon as possible. These pests are typically a quarter of an inch in size and can come in green, yellow, pink, black or gray varieties.

Aphids like to feed on the juices of the plant and you can find them chewing on stems, leaves, buds, fruits or roots. They are particularly drawn to the newest parts of the plant. If you find that your leaves are misshapen or yellowing, checking the bottom can reveal aphids. They also leave behind a sticky substance referred to as honeydew. This sweet substance can actually attract other kinds of pests so aphids are particularly annoying little critters. This substance can also lead to the growth of fungus, like sooty mold which can cause your branches or leaves to turn an unpleasant black color. Aphids are also able to carry viruses from one plant to another so they can help nasty pathogens to spread quicker.

Like spider mites, spraying water on the leaves can dislodge them and leave them with a hard time finding their way back to your plants. If the infestation is large, dusting your plants with flour can constipate them and help convince them it is time to move on. Wiping down your plants with a mixture of soapy water can also help to kill and drive them off.

**Thrips**

Like spider mites and aphids, these little guys are also tiny. Often, they are only around 5 millimeters long. It can be hard to spot these little guys but they leave damage that is clear as day.

If you start to see little metallic black specks on your leaves, you probably have some thrips snacking off your garden. Leaves that thrips attack will often turn brown and become super dry because the thrips like to suck out their juices.

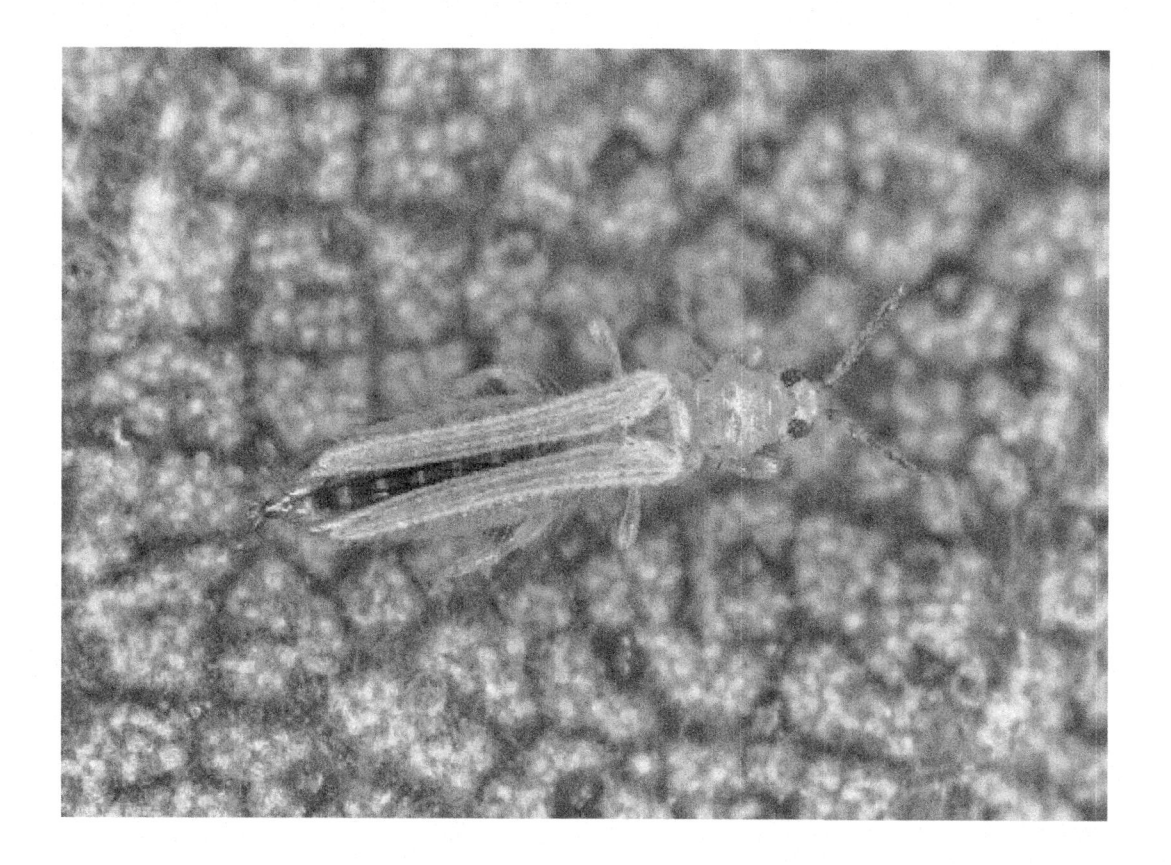

Thrips are small and are either black or the color of straw. They have slender bodies and two pairs of wings. Because they are so small, they look like dark threads to the naked eye. They like to feed in large groups and will fly away if you disturb them.

They stick their eggs into flowers and leaves and they only take a couple of days to hatch so a thrip infestation can feel like it just happened out of the blue.

Because thrips like to lay their eggs in plants, it is super important that you remove any dead or fallen plant matter. If you paid attention in the last chapter, you'll know you should be doing this anyway as it helps to prevent many issues that can assail our hydroponic gardens. Make sure that you inspect your plants for thrip damage and remove any that are infested. Hosing off the plants will also help to reduce their population. Ladybugs, lacewings and minute pirate bugs all feed on thrips and can be beneficial to your garden.

**Fungus Gnats**

Fungus gnats are an odd one. Adult fungus gnats have no interest in harming your garden. But their larvae enjoy chewing on the roots of your plants which slows growth and opens the plant up for infection. In extreme cases, fungus gnat larvae can actually cause the death of plants.

They really like areas with a lot of moisture and a high humidity. You'll likely notice adult fungus gnats before you have any issue.

As adults, these gnats are about three millimeters in length and kind of look like mosquitos. They tend to be a grayish- black color with a pair of long legs and clear wings. Their larvae have shiny black heads with a whitish-transparent body.

Adults typically live for a week and in that time lay up to 300 eggs. It takes half a week for the larvae to emerge but when they do, they start a two-week diet where their main dish is the roots of your plants. When they feed on your plants, they cause them to wilt, stunt their growth and cause a yellowing of their leaves. These nasty little things can have many generations living off the same plant.

If you suspect a fungus gnat infestation than you should inspect your plants by carefully turning up the soil around their stems and look for larvae. If you check a plant and it suddenly let's loose a bunch of adult gnats then you should dispose of that plant. They really like damp soils so make sure you aren't overwatering your plants. If you have a fungus gnat problem then letting your potting medium drain longer will help to kill off the larvae and mess up the development of fungus gnat eggs.

You can also spray your plants with a combination of peppermint, cinnamon and sesame oils. This mixture is called flying insect killer and will help to get rid of gnats.

## Whiteflies

About the same size as spider mites, whiteflies look like small white moths that take up residence on your plants. They are easier to spot but because they fly away when you bother them they can be hard to kill.

Like aphids, they enjoy sucking the juices out of your plant and you see their damage as white spots and yellowing of the leaves.

They tend to lay 200-400 eggs in clusters on the underside of the higher leaves. These eggs hatch in about a week and unattractive little nymphs come out that crawl around on your leaves before they grow wings.

These crawlers will spread out from the egg and find a place to start chewing on your leaves.

They'll stay in that spot for the next week or so before growing into young adults which will repeat the cycle of movement-feasting.

Ladybugs and lacewings enjoy eating whiteflies and so introducing them to your garden can help to kill off whitefly populations. Hosing off plants with a strong blast of water will help in reducing their numbers as well. There are a bunch of organic pesticides on the market which you can get to deal with whiteflies. These pesticides can also work for the other pests but pesticides should be a last resort option, one that you are careful with so as not to lead to undue stress on your plants.

## Preventing Pests

Now that we have an idea of the pests that are most common to hydroponic gardens, let us turn our attention towards how we prevent these pests from getting into our gardens in the first place. Many of these techniques will help us to identify a possible infestation as it is trying to get started and so they offer us early warnings to prepare ourselves to battle pests. If we keep up our preventative measures and keep our eyes peeled for pests then we can save our plants a lot of damage and ourselves a lot of time by cutting off the problem at the head.

When it comes to pests it is also important to understand that not every pest is the same. This doesn't just mean that whiteflies are different from fungus gnats. What this means is that fungus gnats on the West coast are going to be different than fungus gnats on the East coast. Not every solution for prevention or extermination will work. A certain pesticide may be used to kill gnats on the East but the ones on the West might have grown an immunity to it. For this reason, it is important to check with your local hydroponics store to see if there is any region-specific information you need to tackle your pest problem.

One of the ways that we prevent pests is to make sure that we limit their ability to enter our garden in the first place. We can do this a few ways. Insect screens go a long way to keeping out pests. We also want to limit the amount of traffic in and around our setups. If at all possible, our setups will benefit greatly if they can be protected by airlock entrances as these offer the most secure protection against both pests and pathogens. Airlocks can be doubled up to create a space before the garden in which to wipe down dirt and any insects or eggs that are catching a free ride on your clothing.

In order to see if pests are starting to show up in your garden, use sticky traps around your plants. Yellow and blue sticky traps are both useful, as they attract different pests, so you want to make sure to use both kinds for the best results. Place traps near any entrances into your garden such as doors or ventilation systems. Also, make sure to place one or two near the stems of your plants to catch those pests that prefer snacking on the lower bits, such as aphids or fungus gnats. Get into the habit of checking these traps regularly as they can give you a great idea of what kind of life is calling your garden home.

While traps will help us to get a head start fighting any infections, they aren't a foolproof method when it comes to avoiding pests. Traps should be used together with personal spot checks. This means that you should be checking your plants for pests a couple of times a week. Take a clean cloth and check the bottom of your leaves.

Check around the roots for any fungus gnat larvae. You can check the tops of leaves visually. Look for any signs of yellowing or bite marks as described above.

Make sure to remove any weeds that take up root in your garden as these plants are only going to sap your garden's resources and offer a breeding ground for pests. Also remove dead or fallen plant matter, of course. This includes leaves but also any fruit, buds or petals that have been dropped.

Finally, before you introduce any new plants to your garden, make sure to quarantine them first so that you can check them for pests. You can use a magnifying glass to get a closer look if you need to. Give the new plants a thorough inspection, making sure to check all parts of the plant and the potting soil before you transfer it over.

By creating a system and a schedule for inspecting your plants, you can prevent an infestation of pests from ruining your garden or causing you a lot of headaches. A vigilant eye will give you the upper hand in both preventing and dealing with any kind of problem you have with pests. Remember, a strong defense is the best offense when it comes to keeping your plants healthy and free from harm.

## Common Hydroponic Diseases

Disease is awful whether we're speaking about humans or about our plants. In the last chapter, we saw how we maintain a healthy garden so as to prevent pathogens from taking hold in our systems. Here we will look at the most common diseases that hydroponic growers find themselves facing.

## Iron Deficiency

When your plants don't get enough iron they won't be able to produce enough chlorophyll. This means that their leaves will turn bright yellow with bold green veins. If left untreated, the leaves will start to turn white and then begin to die. This will result in a stunting of growth and a dying back of the plant as a whole. These signs of iron deficiency look a lot like some of the other diseases so it is important that you confirm it is an iron deficiency before you begin treatment.

To diagnose an iron deficiency, you are going to want to test your growing operation. Do a pH test and check the numbers. Higher than 7.0 can cause many plants to stop absorbing iron. Also, do an EC reading and check your levels; you may have an imbalance. Remember that an EC check doesn't confirm how many of each nutrient is in your solution so you may consider changing out the nutrient solution for a freshly balanced batch.

If you have identified an iron deficiency, the first thing you should do is fix the pH and EC levels and get that all within the proper range. You can also buy liquid iron which you use to spray down your plants. Spray the liquid iron directly on the leaves. Liquid iron is only a quick fix and not the solution, so if it shows results then consider tweaking your nutrient solution to include more iron.

**Powdery Mildew**

Powdery mildew is an easily recognizable fungal disease. Caused by fungal species, this disease thrives on plants in areas with less moisture in the growing medium and it especially loves it when the humidity levels are high on the surface of your plants. This mildew begins on the younger leaves of plants and it looks like little blisters all over them. These blisters are slightly raised and they lead to your leaves curling up. This curling exposes the lower parts of the leaf's structure for easier access. Leaves that have been infected look like they are coated in an unsightly white powder. Left untreated the leaves will turn brown and fall off. It primarily attacks new leaves and so the older, more mature leaves of your plant will tend to be free of infection.

To deal with powdery mildew, you want to prune away some of the plant to open it up to better airflow. This will help to reduce the humidity of the plant so as to make it less inviting to powdery mildew. Remove any foliage that is already infected and make sure to clean up any fallen plant matter. A spray made of 60% water and 40% milk can be used once every two weeks to help prevent powdery mildew from taking hold.

Also wash your plants from time to time, as this will help prevent both powdery mildew and a variety of pests. A fungicide can be applied if the problem is extreme but this also risks hurting the plants.

**Gray Mold**

Gray mold goes by a variety of names such as ash mold or ghost spot. Regardless of the name you call it, you can spot it easily. It begins as little gray spots on your plants that start to turn into a fuzzy gray abrasion that eats away at your plant until it's entirely brown and nothing more than a disgusting mush. Gray mold can be found on a bunch of plants but it is particularly familiar to anyone that has grown strawberries as it completely ruins the berries it infects.

Gray mold likes to settle in near the bottom of the plant and in the areas that the plant shadows the most. It tends to begin on flowers that have wilted and then it quickly spreads out to the leaves and stem. It really likes those areas with a high humidity. The infected plants will begin to rot away and if left untreated, gray mold is one of the most disgusting diseases to have to deal with. The spores like cool temperatures and high humidity and they can get into the healthy tissue of the plants directly so your plants are especially susceptible after a trimming.

Pruning your plants or setting up on with a trellis helps to improve the air circulation and lower the humidity of your plants so that gray mold will desire them less. You can also use a small fan to increase the airflow around your plants. Always remove any fallen plant matter. If you spray your plants down in the morning, give them time to dry so that gray mold is less interested in the bed. Fungicides can also help in tackling gray mold infections.

**Preventing Disease**

We saw in the last chapter how we maintain our hydroponic gardens. These steps are also important because they help us to prevent disease from taking hold in our gardens. Because they are directly related to our conversation here in this chapter, you will recognize a lot of this information.

However, it is of vital importance in keeping disease out of your garden so it is worth restating.

The most important thing we can do to help our plants avoid becoming diseased is to make sure that they are healthy and not overly stressed. This means we want to check our pH and EC levels regularly to make sure that they are in the proper range. We also want to make sure that we clean our reservoir from time to time and have a schedule for cycling out the old solution and filling it back up with a new, freshly balanced one. This will help your plants to stay healthy which helps them to fend off attacks by pathogens.

You also want to keep your garden as clean as possible. Like with pests, using a two-door airlock system will give you an area in which to wipe down and clean up before you enter into the garden. Doing this helps to remove dirt from your person, which is absolutely the leading way for pathogens to get introduced into your setup. Make sure to clean your hands and any tools you plan to use in the garden before you start messing around. Also, clean off your boots and consider removing any jacket or outdoor wear that you have on.

Clean up any spills as soon as they happen to avoid introducing extra moisture and humidity around your plants as these attract disease. Also make sure that you are removing any dead plant matter as soon as you spot it. Dead plant matter becomes a breeding ground for both pests and disease. Check your plants for disease regularly and remove any that show signs of heavy infection. Consider washing your plants down twice a week or so to knock off any pests or infection that may be trying to take hold.

By keeping vigilant and maintaining your garden, you can prevent disease from taking hold and ensure that you are raising healthy, beautiful crops.

In the next chapter, we will look at some of the mistakes that new growers are prone to make and see how we can avoid making them ourselves. We'll also look at some of the myths surrounding hydroponic growing to dispel any false ideas we may still have about it.

# Chapter 7:
# Myths And Mistakes To Avoid

Our time together has almost come to a close. Before you go out and get going on your own garden, let us take the time to look at some of the mistakes and myths that pop up frequently in discussions on hydroponic gardening. By digging through the myths to find the truth and learning from the mistakes of those that came before us, we are able to benefit from the knowledge and avoid making the same mistakes ourselves.

**Mistake: Hard-to-Use Setups**

When you are setting up your hydroponic garden, it is important that you consider how hard it will be to use. Are you going to have a difficult time reaching the plants in the back because you put the garden up against a wall? Are you going to bump into the lights every time you try to tend the bed because the space is too small and cramped?

When you are setting up your garden it is important that you consider issues such as the physical space in which it will sit. You want to make sure that you can get to all your plants without a struggle. If you're knocking over lights or throwing your back out to reach plants then the setup isn't going to be a very good one. Chances are you are going to end up breaking something or neglecting it. Consider the ways in which you move through the garden space; make sure that you are able to reach everything.

You also want to make sure that you are able to get to your reservoir easily. While it may be tempting just to rest the grow tray on top of the reservoir, consider how this might cause issues when it comes time to switch the nutrient solution. Will you have somewhere to place the grow tray while you have to mess around with the reservoir? If not, then how did you plan to do it?

We saw in chapter five all the different steps we take to maintain our hydroponic garden. Read those steps again before you set up your garden and

make sure that your setup allows you to actually get in the garden and take those actions. If not, then you will want to reconsider your design.

## Myth: Hydroponic Gardens Are Only for Illegal Substances

It seems that any time hydroponics pop up in the news it is in relation to some illegal grow operation that has been busted by the police. This has led to a stigma around hydroponics, one which it really doesn't deserve. Just because it happens that a lot of illegal growers use hydroponic setups, it doesn't mean that hydroponics is used just for illegal purposes.

As we saw above, we went an entire book looking at hydroponics and never once did we mention any drugs. We looked at how hydroponics will help our herb gardens to produce 30% more aromatic oils. We talked about vegetables and fruits. Never once did we speak about illegal substances.

This is because hydroponics is a system for growing plants. Those plants don't need to be illegal. They can be, yes. But they can also be the garden veggies you serve in a salad. Hydroponics is just a great system for growing plants and it is a system that you can run from inside your house, which means that you can hide your garden easily. But hydroponics itself is not illegal, it does not mean that you are taking part in illegal activities and this particular myth should be put to rest already.

## Mistake: Choosing the Wrong Crops for Your Climate

You hear about a new crop on one of the gardening sites you check online. It sounds like it could be a lot of fun to grow, some kind of berry you never heard of before and people say it does great in a hydroponic setup. You order some seeds, plant it and it grows but it just doesn't give the results you wanted. Looking to see what goes wrong, you do some more Googling on the plant and you realize it needs to be in a super-hot, arid environment. And you're living through the coldest winter of your life.

Different plants want different climates and nothing will be more disappointing than trying to grow a plant that just doesn't like the climate you can offer. We should always do our research on the plants that we want to grow.

We can do this easily with Google or by going into our local hydroponic store to speak to the staff.

## Myth: Hydroponics Have to be Done Indoors

We've spoken a lot about indoor hydroponics in this book. This was a choice to highlight the fact that we can raise hydroponics indoors. There any many people out there who don't have access to an outside plot in which to start a garden. Most people that live in an apartment building have at best a balcony and many don't even have that much. Being that you can have an indoor garden, hydroponics offers a way for more people to get into gardening.

But this doesn't mean that you can't have an outdoor hydroponic garden. When we raise our gardens indoors, we are able to control the seasons and really take an active role in maintaining the humidity and temperature, how long the grow lights are on and much more. If we grow outdoors then we can save money on grow lights by using the sun but we also open our garden up to more risk from pests and disease. However, hydroponics can be done anywhere that you want.

## Mistake: Picking the Wrong Plants for Your Setup

This could also be called "Not Doing Your Research." Like picking plants that match your climate, you are also going to want to make sure you pick plants that will work well in your setup. Some plants work better in different systems. Some want less water; some want slower draining and others want more water and others yet want faster draining. It is important that you research the plants that you want to put in your garden. There are hundreds upon hundreds of websites jam-packed with information about every plant you could consider growing. They will tell you the pH and EC levels for the plant, how hot they like their environment, how much water they want and what type of hydroponic setup is best for them. We looked at a handful throughout this book but there is no way we could have covered all of them. But Google is your friend. So make sure you do your research and plan out your garden. Preparing yourself with information will avoid costly mistakes. Not only does it cost to grow but there is also a time cost and you will lose weeks before you realize that growing that one plant is a losing battle.

## Myth: Hydroponics is Super Expensive

This myth has good reason to be around. The truth is that hydroponics can be expensive. Can be. But just because it can be doesn't mean that it always is. When you head to the hydroponic store and look at all the prices and get talked into buying more than you really needed, then it is going to be expensive. But like many hobbies, it depends on how serious you want to take it and you can always start slow.

There are a ton of ways to cut down costs when beginning your garden. Searching online you can find hundreds of do-it-yourself guides to starting a hydroponic setup. We looked at three pretty cheap options ourselves in chapter two. These offer great ways to try out hydroponic gardening for the new grower. You can get your hands dirty and really see if it is something that you enjoy before you go spending a lot of money. Speaking of spending a lot of money...

## Mistake: Scaling Up the Operation Too Early

Starting off too big can be a terrible mistake. For one, it means sinking a lot of money into growing right out the gate. Before you do this you should at least have some experience with hydroponics. Another big issue is that until you have some experience you don't actually know how to best care for your garden and every step in the operation cycle is going to be a learning experience. This isn't bad when we start small but starting bigger means any mistakes we make along the way are going to cost us that much more.

You should start slow and learn the ropes. As you go along you can buy more expensive equipment as you figure out what equipment you actually need and what equipment works best with your style of growing. As you learn the way your plants take to the system, get a feel for how they grow in your setup, then you can begin to expand.

You can start to add in another grow tray, maybe two. But add slowly, take your time and make sure you have a good grasp of how to run a small garden before you jump into a large one. You can always get there but patience will help save you from some truly devastating mistakes along the way. It's one thing to mess up one grow tray, it's another to mess up a dozen.

## Myth: Hydroponics is Unnatural

What happened to just sticking a plant in the ground and letting it grow? Hydroponics seems like a lot of work to do the same thing. The plants come out bigger, too. Seems like there must be something unnatural going on here. It must be all those chemicals used in the solution.

Of course, this myth is just silly. We are growing plants and using natural mix in our grow trays. We mix together a nutrient solution but all of these are natural nutrients that the plants take from the Earth anyway. Hydroponics is just a system of growing. We grow healthy plants the same as any gardener tries to. There are no gross chemicals being used to give us better growth than soil. All we are doing is using the natural desires of the plant to provide it with the most comfortable growing experience we can.

In a way, hydroponics is almost like owning a pet. There are wild dogs in the world but nobody thinks it is unhealthy to have a pet dog. We are treating our plants the same; we are providing for their needs so that they can focus on living. Just in the case of plants, living means growing into fruit or vegetables that we can enjoy afterward!

## Mistake: Not Maintaining Your Garden

I know, I know. You've heard this one before. But it is the number one mistake that new growers make and so we are going to speak about it one last time. The fact is that maintaining your garden doesn't just mean changing the water. It doesn't just mean we look at the garden when the plants look ill and infected and get to work. Maintaining our gardens is a commitment that any gardener has to honor.

Something spill? Better wipe that up. There's dead plant matter in your grow tray or on the floor around your setup? Best clean that up and get rid of it. Infestations and infections love to grow in these conditions. So, check your plants, test the water, clean up the beds and show them a little love. You wouldn't let your dog sleep in its own waste, so why would you let your plants? Maintaining your garden is the most important thing you can do as a new grower.

Treat your plants right.

## Mistake: Forgetting to Have Fun

If you are growing because you want to sell your crops, that's a fine reason to do it. But try to have fun. For many, this is an enjoyable hobby and brings them a lot of peace. When you start to get money involved, it can be easy to lose track of that. Don't forget to take time to smell the roses. Or the tomatoes, whatever it is you're growing.

**JAMIE BACKYARD**

# Conclusion

We've come a long way throughout the course of this book. Starting with a definition of hydroponics, we're covered a lot of information that will help you to get started on your own hydroponic garden. Before we close, let's go over a brief summary of what we covered and share some words on where to go from here.

Hydroponics has been around for literally ages but it is only just starting to pick up some serious interest. These gardens can take a bit of work to set up and maintain but they offer a great way of growing crops.

We focused here on those looking to get started with hydroponics, so we tailored our information towards the beginner. The lessons we covered, however, have everything the beginner needs to get started and begin the road to expert.

We have six primary setups to choose from when it comes to what kind of system we want to set up. We saw how to set up deep water, wicking and drip systems. These are the easiest systems for DIY setups and beginners but there are also aeroponics, ebb and flow and nutrient film technique systems.

These systems are more complicated than is recommended for a beginner but I encourage you to research these more as you get more comfortable with hydroponics.

There are four key elements that we looked at as the operation cycle of the hydroponic garden. These are soiling, seeding, lighting and trimming. By understanding how each of these elements works, we are able to handle the growing cycle of our plants. There are many options available for soiling and several for lighting. Finding the combination that is right for you will take some research but it should ultimately be decided on what plants you want to grow.

Speaking of plants, we have seen that there are a ton of plants that work really well in hydroponic gardens. Herbs grown in a hydroponic garden have 30% more aromatic oils than those grown in soil. Lettuce in particular absolutely adores growing hydroponically. Each plant has its own preferences when it comes to how much water it wants, the pH level it likes best and the temperature that it needs to grow. For this reason, we have to research our plants and make sure that we only grow those that are compatible together.

We also learned how to mix our own nutrient solutions so that we can provide our plants with what they need to grow. There are a lot of pre-mixed options available for purchase as well.

Taking control of our own mix is just another way we are able to get closer to our plants and provide for them to the best of our ability.

The importance of maintaining a clean garden cannot be stressed enough and so we spent time learning how we care for our gardens. The information in chapter five can be used to build your own maintenance schedule. To do this, look at how often each step of maintenance needs to be performed and plan ahead so that you don't forget. It's super important that we take care of our plants because we don't want them in dirty environments nor do we want them to be overly stressed. A dirty environment and a stressed plant are a recipe for infestation and infection.

We explored some of the most common pests that attack our plants. However, we didn't cover all of them. That would take a whole book. The pests we covered are the most likely ones you will have to deal with but that doesn't mean they will be the only ones. It is a good thing we also learned how to prevent pests. The preventive steps we learned will also help us to spot any pests we did not cover. If you find something you don't recognize in one of your traps then you know it's time for more research. Remember too that not every insect is a pest, some help us out by eating pests!

Infection is a risk with all gardens and so our number one tool in preventing harmful pathogens from attacking our plants is to make sure that our plants are nice and strong. We clean our gardens, we provide them with nutrients mixed to their liking, we give them the love and care they need and in doing this we keep them healthy and unstressed. While infection can still take hold in a healthy plant, it is far more likely to attack stressed plants. This preventative step combines what we learned in chapter six about pests and infection with the skills we practice in chapter five.

Finally, we looked at mistakes that are common to beginning hydroponic gardeners. We also exploded those myths that surround hydroponics to dispel the lies and untruths surrounding our newfound hobby. Searching online for tips or mistakes will reveal many discussions with hydroponic gardeners that are written specifically to help beginners like you to have the easiest, most enjoyable time possible getting into this form of gardening.

If you're excited to get started then I suggest you begin planning out your garden now. You will need to dedicate a space for it and pick which system is most appealing to you and your skill level. Write down the plants you are most interested in growing and begin gathering information about them; what environment do they like best? What temperature? How much light do they need? What pH level?

Once you know what plants you want to grow and what system you want, you can start to build a shopping list. Along with the hardware to set up the system itself, don't forget to get some pH testing kits and an EC meter. Also make sure you have cleaning material, as you know now how important it is to sanitize and sterilize your equipment. This is also a great time to build your maintenance schedule.

Once you have this information you can return to this book and use it as a manual for walking through every step of the growing process. The information that we covered will take you from beginner and, along with the application of practice, turn you into a pro in no time. But most importantly, don't forget to have fun!

**JAMIE BACKYARD**

# Hydroponic Garden

Discover How to Build an Inexpensive Garden at Home Even if You Are a Beginner. The Ultimate DIY Hydroponics System for Homegrown Organic Fruit, Herbs and Vegetables

By:

**Jamie Backyard**

**JAMIE BACKYARD**

# TABLE OF CONTENTS

Chapter 1: What Is Hydroponic Gardening?......................144

Chapter 2: Herbs, Fruits And Vegetables For Hydroponic Gardening..................................................................150

Chapter 3: Let's Start With Hydroponic Gardening............174

Chapter 4: Common Problems ........................................204

Chapter 5: Tips For Growing Healthy Plants.......................218

Conclusion.......................................................................222

**JAMIE BACKYARD**

# Chapter 1:
# What Is Hydroponic Gardening?

**W**hen we talk about hydroponic gardening, we are talking about a specific technique or branch within a bigger field: hydroculture.

Hydroculture comprises of any technique where plants are grown without any soil at all. This method is fairly old, as we have seen mentioned by Francis Bacon but like all stories, things are not as simple as they appear at first sight.

So, is growing water lentils a form of hydroculture? Of course, it is, as it is growing spirulina (which, by the way, has amazing health benefits and it is a "superfood" if you want to branch out that way). The fact is that some plants, like water lentils, can grow without soil naturally. So, the term "hydroculture" is as large as it is fairly useless to someone who wants to grow their lettuce and tomatoes at home.

Enter two new branches: hydroponics and aquaponics. These are basically two subcategories of hydroculture, and never even try to ask a hydroculture gardener about which is better: the debate is as animated and lively as the old "cats vs. dogs" debate with pet lovers.

We can, however, try to see the factual differences and advantages and disadvantages of both.

Let's start with aquaponics: this is a way of growing plants in the water where there is a whole ecosystem within and around the water pool that will provide the nutrients your plants need.

So, when we talk about aquaponics, we are talking about having a pool with fish, insect larvae, frogs, etc. that will organically produce the food your plants need.

Hydroponics, on the other hand, is when you provide a solution of water and nutrients to your plants. The key concept is to dissolve nutrients in water so that your plants can dip their roots in it and feed themselves.

There are other elements (like keeping the roots oxygenated for example), which we will see later on, but the basic concept is this.

Do not worry about the term "solution"; it sounds chemical, and it does come from chemistry, but a solution can be water and salt, it does not need to include "dangerous chemicals". All the nutrients your plants need can be sourced fully organically; we are talking about minerals like nitrogen, carbon, potassium, magnesium, iron, and calcium. These are simple molecules that you can easily source from nature without any chemical processes that can harm the environment.

So, what are the advantages of hydroponics over aquaponics? Let's see:

To start with, hydroponics is easy! Yes, it is much easier to add the necessary nutrients to a water system to feed your plants than it is to establish a full food chain, habitat and microclimate that will sustain your plants.

This means that hydroponics is easily accessible to amateurs.

Hydroponics can fit in a very small space, while to have an aquaponics garden large enough to be self-sufficient you will need a much larger garden.

You will now think, "But how much water will I need to grow hydroponic plants? Surely a lot!" Actually no... Because the water you use is recycled, hydroponics uses only 10% of the water you would need if you grew your crops conventionally in the soil!

This means that compared to traditional soil gardening, hydroponics will also mean saving on your water bills.

There are, however, a few things that you will need to pay attention to:

With hydroponics, you will have to keep an eye on the nutrients in your water and keep replenishing them.

With hydroponics you will also need to keep your water oxygenated; there won't be any algae that produce oxygen for the roots of your plants as you have in aquaponics.

You will not have fish swimming around in your tanks.

Apart from these, hydroponics is, on the whole, much more popular than aquaponics, and the only real option you have if you want to grow your veggies at home but you do not have any land.

What does the word "hydroponics" mean?

Talking of origins of this technique, where does the term "hydroponics" come from? The word was first used in 1937 by a gentleman called William Frederick Gericke, who was a researcher at the University of California at Berkeley and a pioneer in the field, who used to Greek words to form a new English word: he joined "hydro" which means "water" as you may know with "ponos" which means "work, labor" to give us our word. It is a good description of how hydroponics, as all the work is done by the water. Ok, you will have to do a bit yourself, but nothing compared to what water does.

Why is conventional soil gardening no longer viable?

What is the huge difference between conventional soil gardening and hydroponics?

Even before you look at your dimension and life, we should pay some attention to what conventional agriculture is causing around the world. Since the 1950s in particular, agriculture has become a full-on industrial process.

The agricultural revolution that took place after the Second World War was based on a few key concepts:

The mechanization of labor, which has caused job losses, but also poured a lot of carbon dioxide and other gases into the atmosphere.

Vast monoculture fields, often accompanied by a limited choice of varieties that best suited such production. This has had appalling effects on biodiversity and the ecosystem, for example, by destroying those "corridors" like hedges and small woods that small animals use to move from one place to another.

Using chemically produced fertilizers; this has meant pollution all round, from the production of fertilizers to the soil they fertilize. But it has also caused soil impoverishment.

Using chemical herbicides (or weed killers); this has reduced biodiversity and polluted beyond any sustainable level.

Using chemical pesticides; this too has polluted and destroyed the ecosystem.

All this was with the promise that we would one day feed the entire world yet people are still starving, not because we don't produce enough.

We produce enough for 10 billion people, but because industrial farming methods also meant a distribution controlled by big corporations that fleece you off in supermarkets and allow hundreds of millions of people to starve.

# Chapter 2:
# Herbs, Fruits And Vegetables For Hydroponic Gardening

For the hydroponic cultivation are very many different plants such as herbs, salads, and vegetables, berries, but also edible flowers and flowers. The size of the plants, whether hanging or standing, as well as the required lighting conditions, must be taken into account when growing the plants and selecting the hydroponic system.

Herbs feel good in hydroponics, grow very well, and you can grow many herbs in a small space. If one considers the demands on the sun, partial shade or shade and keeps an eye on the water-nutrient mixture, as in the traditional cultivation in soil, one can rejoice over an abundant harvest. Regular pruning also promotes plant growth here. The list shows herbs that are well suited for hydroponic cultivation. You can grow almost all plants hydroponically, except root vegetables. Fast- growing varieties, such as pak choi, Asia salad, or swiss chard, are interesting, as they can be harvested frequently. But also, many other vegetables quickly deliver high yields and taste very good. The list shows examples of which vegetables can be cultured hydroponically.

## Valerian

Valerian is an herbaceous plant that originates in central Europe and Asia but is now widespread also in western Europe and North America. The valerian develops very broadly and can reach a height of one and a half meters. The rhizome of the valerian plant is composed of many roots that are characterized by an unpleasant smell. The typical environment of the valerian is the areas rich in humidity, the margins of the courses of the rivers, woods, etc.. However, we can cultivate it very well even in our gardens when it has no particular needs. The optimal climate for the cultivation of valerian is the temperate one, however, this plant can withstand even temperatures of fifteen degrees below zero; likes sun exposure but also semi-shaded. Valerian is multiplied by seed, by the division of the rhizome or tuft. Before proceeding with sowing, the soil will be worked deeply. If seed multiplication is chosen, it will be done during the spring period starting from the seedbed; this operation takes a long time because the valerian has a very slow development.

## Basil

Basil is one of the most cultivated aromatic plants in Italy; in fact, it is a small herbaceous plant, native to Asia, which came to Europe centuries ago, and has been cultivated both in Europe and in Asia for a very long time. In fact, the basil we are used to eating and seeing in the garden is a hybrid plant, whose botanical name is ocimum basilicum "Genoese", testimony to the city where the use of basil is more widespread. It is a perennial plant, generally cultivated as an annual, as it fears the cold, and temperatures below 10°C cause its rapid deterioration. Basil, as we know it, is just one of several varieties spread in cultivation; in fact, in the Italian kitchen we particularly appreciate the so-called sweet basil, with a large leaf and a delicate aroma.

## Borage

Borage alias cucumber. Borage has a taste of fresh green cucumber, which makes it excellent in salads or on spreads. In medicine, the seeds of the plant or the borage oil derived from it are used mainly for skin complaints.

## Watercress

Watercress, also called bach or watercress, botanically belongs to the family brassica (Brassicaceae). In addition to the genuine watercress (nasturtium officinale), the small-leaved watercress (nasturtium microphyllum) is very common in Germany. The original range of the two species probably extended over Europe, north Africa, and southwest Asia. Meanwhile, watercress as a neophyte, however, can be found almost worldwide. It likes to settle on shady, clear, shallow waters with a slight current, for example, at sources or in the shallow riparian zones of clean streams. Watercress is a beautiful water plant for gardens: it does not only look pretty, but it is also delicious. Watercress: location, and cultivation.

Watercress is a marsh and aquatic plant and thrives best in water depths of 5 to 20 centimeters. It is, therefore, quite expensive to grow them in gardens.

A natural source of water is best for planting watercress. Which makes it suitable for hydroponics. It often grows in nature at the edge of small streams and moats.

You can grow watercress in the pot by pressing the seeds lightly on the ground and keeping them moist. At a temperature of 20 degrees, the seeds begin to germinate after about a week. If the young plants have reached a height of 8 to 10 centimeters, you can put them at the appropriate watering place.

The true watercress was already in ancient times as a medicinal plant cultured. Due to its high vitamin c content, the plant was especially valued as an anti-scurvy. It is also considered a blood purifier. Its name derives from the Latin name "nasus tortus", a twisted nose in English - an expression that results from the reaction to the consumption of the slightly pungent cress type.

The cultivation of watercress is worthwhile not only because of the beautiful sight, but it is also extremely healthy: watercress is rich in vitamins c, a, k, and b2 and was, therefore, one of the few foods in the winter months against scurvy. In addition, it contains iodine, iron, and calcium, as well as mustard oils. They provide a slightly pungent taste and have an antibacterial and digestive effect.

In natural medicine, the fresh leaves of watercress are recommended as a home remedy for cystitis and congested respiratory tract and to stimulate digestion and kidney activity.

# Angelica

The angelica is one of the few medicinal plants that are native to northern Europe and from the north - Greenland and Iceland - by planting in the medieval monastery gardens in the 14th century. Central Europe has become their habitat. For about 500 years, the effects of this magnificent and stately plant in herbal books are described. The spectrum ranges from folk medicine to modern phytotherapy, from the protection against a plague disease to the magenta therapeutic. Its manifold application in the past has brought the angelica also many more names, so we find for them names such as butterbur, theraminwurz, brustwurz, heiliggeistwurz, according to their preferred use. In the alpine region, we often find the wild angelica or waldengelwurz - angelica sylvestris l.

Although it also reaches a height of more than one meter and is thus an attractive umbelliferae in the landscape From these effects, the following fields of application for this aromatic amarum (bitter agent) can be derived: loss of appetite can thus be favorably influenced; if dyspeptic symptoms and mild gastrointestinal spasms are present, these can be well removed with preparations from the root of the angelica. Often, feelings of fullness and bloating are triggered by stressful situations that also respond well to this medicinal plant. In addition to the medicinal use of the angelica root, it is also processed in herb schnapps, liqueurs, and another digestive (digestive preparations); but also, the seasoning of sauces, salads, and other foods is the tart aroma of angelica. The flower stems of the plant are used for candying and thus form a sweet variation in Austrian pastry art.

# Fennel

Fennel is native to the Mediterranean but is now grown worldwide. There are various sub-forms, of which the seeds and the fennel green are used for seasoning or the fennel tuber as vegetables.

Fennel has a sweet, aniseed taste. The leaves and tubers are used, especially in the Mediterranean cuisine for fish and salads. The seeds spice soups, sauces, grilled meat, and fish, but also taste in bread and cake in alcoholic drinks such as pastis or absinthe, fennel rounds off the taste of anise.

Fennel needs warm and sunny locations with light, not too moist soil; it is relatively sensitive. As medicinal plant fennel has many effects: it helps against flatulence and abdominal pain, in diseases of the upper respiratory tract and as an infusion against eye pain and inflamed eyelids.

## Strawberries

Hydroponics technical system that allows the greenhouse cultivation of fruit and vegetables on a sluggish substrate or not, by optimally managing the elements that determine the quality of the plants and the product: temperature, irrigation, light, etc.

The hydroponics in general and the strawberry, in particular, allows to improve all the elements responsible for the quality of the plant and the final product, through higher production and higher quality, u the solution to the problems arising from the culture soil (dirt, slowness, fungi, mold...) And standardization of production. Hydroponics strawberries can also be adopted for smaller plants, such as home, thanks to the cost rather than content and ease of installation.

In the fruit and vegetable sector, the introduction of strawberry technology

was favoured by specific structural and ecological conditions of this crop: in recent years, the cultivation of strawberries also encountered rapid development, moving from classical cultivation in open land cultivation land substrate and especially bags of peat.

With hydroponics, strawberries are constantly kept in optimal nutritional conditions, because the techniques used guarantee phytosanitary conditions best and cleanest product. The result is higher quality strawberries, with a better look, a consistent size, inherent properties better to endure (less crude fibre content, higher percentage of sugar fats, vitamins, a higher density), lower availability and increased capacity of long-distance transport.

Cultivated strawberries are hydroponically protected by the adoption of different types of tunnels, depending on the investment cost and depreciation, openings of have been tested and afford by the side or side and is usually made of plastic films each takes an average of 3-4 years, with average brightness and good thermal insulation properties. Grow bags can be placed in a set of files of pedestals or hung in the height of the structure, which can be useful to receive the product in the palms of individual farmers. Strawberry plants are planted in plastic bags (from 4 to 6 per bag) of 10-12 litres per lot, with sizes of 20-25 cm width 35-40 cm long. The contents of the bags are usually made of white peat and pear in a variable portion.

However, there are many types of hydroponics for the production of strawberries that reach each other for how the water reaches the roots of the plant.

## Cucumbers

Hydroculture for cucumbers with your own hands will be very welcome in the economy if you want to get a good harvest of this vegetable quickly. Cucumbers are climbers, so it is better in small hydroponics to sow them along the wall of the pallet, and after the shoots appear, bind them to the installed at an angle stops. This method helps breeders looking for a way to grow cucumbers quickly. Such placement of cucumbers does not disturb other plants that may also be in this range, and the bound cucumbers eventually produce fruits of much higher quality. Optimal growth of cucumbers contributes to the bright day up to 14 hours.

## Varieties of cucumbers for growing in hydroponics

The most popular cucumbers for hydroponic cultivation are "European" or "long English" cucumbers. Beit alpha (ba), Japanese or Persian varieties are becoming increasingly popular. They are similar to the European cucumbers but are smaller (usually 10-15 cm) and in contrast to the European cucumbers with an average size of 30 to 35 cm. These cucumbers are gutted and have thin skin and do not need to be cleaned when preparing salads. Due to its thin skin, the necessary moisture in the room must be maintained to avoid weight loss. European species - occupy the second place for hydroponic crops with high yields in confined spaces. Unlike tomato plantations, which are more robust, cucumber is more tender. They must be constantly kept under special growth conditions in order to achieve maximum yields. When cucumbers are left unattended, they quickly get entangled, and yields drop dramatically. They are then almost impossible to untangle, unlike tomatoes. Therefore, proper care is required throughout the growth cycle.

## What you need to grow cucumbers in hydroponics

If you want to grow tomatoes and cucumbers in your own cottage, you will need to purchase a hydroponic installation. If the purchase is not possible, you can create it yourself. This requires:
- Expanded clay
- Plastic pipes for further planting

- Pump
- Mineral wool
- Mineral fertilizers
- Compost layer
- Selected medium gravel
- Capacity for plants, mostly glasses
- Water

## The technology of growing cucumbers with hydroponics

Hydroponics will help to cultivate cucumbers in the home, comparable to those grown in the garden. It is necessary to follow the technology of cultivation strictly.

## Sowing seeds in cassettes

First, the cork stoppers are soaked in a nutrient solution; then, a cucumber core is placed in the centre of each cork. Hydroponics contains many nutrients in the solution that help to saturate the seed from within.

Powder vermiculite will help to create an optimal humid environment. After planting, the seeds of the cassette are covered with a plastic wrap, which is removed after 3 days. The temperature to be followed is 23-25 ° c.

## Replanting sprouts into cubes

Cubes, such as cassettes, are subjected to a solution treatment (as described in the article) to prepare a hydroponic solution, after which seven days of shoots can be transferred there. You should take a seedling with a cork and transfer it to a cube to reduce the temperature by 1 degree. The increased distance between the cubes contributes to the normal development of the plants. Sprouting seedlings in such conditions are 1.5 months.

## Transplanting cucumber seedlings in mats

Before you plant cucumbers at home, the mats must be soaked in a solution. Make small holes in the packaging that serve as a drainage function. It should take place at a temperature of +22-25°C. After the beginning of flowering, the seedling forms a stem, after which the fifth leaf must remove all flowers. The germination of the roots in the mat should be done at a temperature of
+21-22 °C.

## Features care for cucumbers

If we have decided to grow cucumbers at home, we have to take good care of them. Before the formation of the first fruit, the stalk must be constantly removed. As the number of cucumbers increases, it is worthwhile to control the transition from vegetative to generative growth.

Cucumbers should be carefully watered, with sprinkling begun 2 hours after sunrise and 2 hours before sunset to avoid deformation of the fruit. The temperature should not exceed + 19-22°C and + 24°C on sunny days. It is necessary to ventilate the greenhouse regularly, maintaining a humidity of 70-80% to avoid mildew and botrytis.

## Advantages and disadvantages of growing cucumbers with hydroponics

The advantages of hydroponics are:
- Fast growth of cucumbers
- Fruit does not accumulate harmful chemicals, which has a positive effect on human health.
- Space saving in a similar type of cultivation,
- If necessary, plants can be transplanted to another location,
- One of the main advantages of the method is that no land is
- needed, which is particularly important in areas with a lack of fertile land.
- Cucumbers do not need to be poured frequently.

There are virtually no disadvantages to this type of cultivation, but there are negative features:
- Spending on equipment
- Performing frequent monitoring of the temperature regime of plants.

## Melons

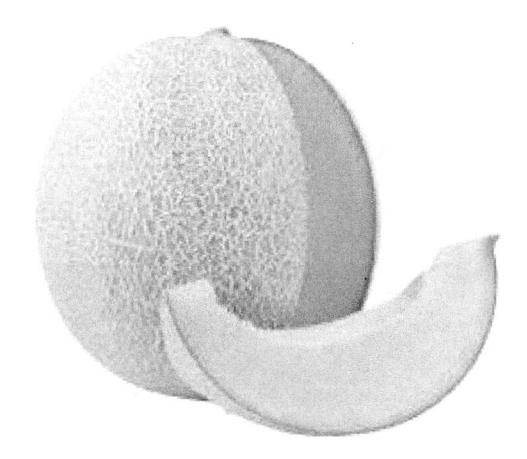

Melons probably come from the subtropical regions of Asia and have been cultivated for millennia. As their botanical name suggests cucumis melo, they are related to the cucumbers. The cucumis melo is distributed as sugar or honeydew melon, cantaloupe melon, and nettle melon. The watermelon (citrullus lanatus) belongs to a different genus. Cantaloupe melons are usually recognized by their firm orange flesh. The shell is hard, scaly, and traversed by longitudinal grooves.

The variety of 'Charentais' is considered precocious. Depending on the variety, honeydew melons have a smooth or ribbed yellow to greenish skin. Inside they are yellowish to white or orange. Net melons can be recognized by the net pattern of the shell. The flesh is green to white or salmon-colored. The fruits of the variety 'hale's best jumbo' can weigh up to two kilograms. Melons germinate at temperatures between 20 and 30 degrees Celsius. Therefore, we recommend that you prefer plants in warm conditions. In April, you can sow the seeds one to two centimetres deep and place them on a warm, sunny windowsill. Our tip: if you sow in small pots, you do not need to pimp them. The plants are sensitive to cold. Therefore, it is best to plant them in the second half of May or early June - ideally in the greenhouse. The distance between the melon plants should be 80 by 80 centimetres.

## Location and care

Melons need a lot of heat. The more sun and heat they get, the better the fruits will grow, and the sweeter and more aromatic they become. Some varieties thrive well in partial shade, as long as it is warm enough.

They also make some demands on the ground. He should be relaxed and nutritious. The best way is to prepare the bed of compost and give them some slow-release fertilizer in the planting hole. Additional fertilizers during the summer need the strong-consuming plants. In addition, you should always pour it sufficiently.

In order for melons to plant many fruits, it is recommended to cut them: cap the main shoot after the fourth or fifth leaf so that its branches. Repeat the procedure for the side shoots after four to eight leaves. The following shoots then form the flowers and later the fruits.

You can pull melons on trellises or spread on the ground. Then put a board under the fruit, so they do not rot.

Melons are considered to be sensitive to fungal diseases such as fusarium wilt. They can also be attacked by powdery mildew and downy mildew.

Harvest and use of melons

Depending on the sowing season and season melons mature from August. Whether you can harvest them, you will recognize by their color and their sweet scent. For some varieties, the stalk dries. It is best to harvest the melons quickly by separating them from the plant with a sharp knife. Overripe fruits do not taste that good anymore.

You can eat melons in the summer just like that. You can also use them for salads, desserts and cold drinks. Since they are not very durable, you eat them right away.

## Tomatoes

Hydroponic seedlings, including tomatoes, are grown in small pots floating or suspended over water so that the tomato roots absorb the necessary amount of nutrient-rich water necessary for the tomatoes or other hydroponic plants to grow. An unsinkable support system must first be built or purchased in order to plant and grow using the hydroponic method.

## Instructions

Purchase hydroponic plant trays for growing tomatoes. Trays with larger holes are used to better support adult tomato plants (remember, if you want to grow the tomatoes completely in the hydroponic beds or pimp them in a garden or pot during the warm growing season).

Use a cutter to cut larger holes in hydroponic plant trays with holes for adult tomato plants too small. Be careful not to let the lower ends taper conically to allow the root system to fall through to provide better watering results.

Purchase or build a waterbed to place the trays. Build the beds of wooden

frames on the inside covered with a single solid sheet or plastic.

Fill the plant tray holes halfway down the ground and drop a tomato seed into each hole. Cover the seeds, fill the tray with holes, and then place in the waterbeds, where the trays remain over water at the surface of the water, with only enough of the tray so that the tomato plant roots can absorb the necessary amount of water.

**Tips and warnings**

Monitor the growth of the plants. Of course, as the plants grow, they will become heavier; if the plants are too heavy to be supported by the trays, you will need to use other materials to support the trays. You do not want to soil the trays by more than an inch deep and risk drowning the root system of the tomatoes. Bricks work to support the shells and prevent them from sinking too deep into the water.

# Cabbage

Cabbage and various related plants are not only used in raw form as food. A feature of this vegetable is the possibility of long storage. Then you can always put on the table a salad of fresh cabbage in the winter season, for example, because tomatoes or cucumbers are grown during this time on hydroponic culture with an incredible amount of chemicals. If you have a backyard or a cottage with a garden, you can grow this salad and not buy it. Caring for cabbage is easy. It is much more important to choose a place for growth. The soil should be fertile; therefore, it is better from autumn to fertilize with cow dung or chicken droppings. At the same time, maximum illumination is required - cabbages are not bound in the shade. The plant needs to be sprayed constantly, especially at the time when the heads are tied. Seed acquisition, therefore, requires clarification as to whether it is early cabbage or late cabbage. On these seedlings hangs and plants in the soil and the frequency of irrigation and the formation of fruits. You cannot plant this vegetable in the soil in which the related plants have grown before it - the harvest will leave much to be desired.

To date, except for traditional cis varieties, white cabbage and red cabbage, there are always brussels and Beijing. These varieties can also be grown beautifully in your garden.

Care for cabbage begins from the moment of germination seed. In the case of brussels sprouts, the seedlings are planted in a greenhouse from March to

May. It does not like land fertilized with fresh fertilizer, so the soil needs to be prepared from autumn. By the way, the sprouts are brussels sprouts. Planting and nursing last from early spring to late autumn when the first frosts come. In May-June, the seedlings are planted on the open ground. During this time, the care of the cabbage requires more time in the opinion of many gardeners. While it does not take root, it is necessary to water it abundantly, fertilize it, fertilize it with fertilizers. By the way, it is important not to overdo it; otherwise, it can come to a later food poisoning. The harvest starts in October. The most valuable and useful are fruits that have fallen in frost. In this case, the protective functions of the plant are activated, releasing many beneficial substances that contribute to improving the well-being of cardiovascular diseases and diabetes. As for the kind of Beijing cabbage -you care for and maintain is not much more difficult than in brussels. It is necessary to sow it in the middle of summer - it is characterized by the rapid formation of head and rifle. It can also be leaf or half root species. In order to preserve an earlier culture, pre-growth of the seedlings is necessary. After the formation of 4-5 mature leaves, the plant is planted in the field. Care for cabbage Beijing during the formation of the head is the same as for any other variety: in the growing season - pest control, loosening beds, watering, and feeding. It is best to use it for cooking salads or borsch. Peking cabbage is well preserved in cellars.

# Chapter 3:
# Let's Start With Hydroponic Gardening

## Grow basil in hydroponic

- Recommended ph: 5 to 6.5
- The plant spacing: 15-25 cm (8-40 plants/m 2)
- The germination time and temperature: 6-7 days with temperature from 20 to 25°C
- The growth time: 5-6 weeks (start harvest when the plant measures 15 cm)
- Temperature: 18-30°C, optimal 20-25°C
- Exposure to light: sunny or slightly sheltered
- Height of the plant and width: 30-70 cm; 30 cm

Recommended aquaponics method: culture beds, nft or dwc
Basil is one of the most popular herbs in aquaponic systems. Particularly in large commercial monoculture units because of its high value and high demand in urban and peri-urban areas. Many basil growers have tried to grow Italian basil, basil lemon and purple basil in their aquaponic systems. Because of its high nitrogen content, basil is an ideal plant in aquaponics. However, care must be taken to avoid excessive depletion of nutrients from the water.

## Growing conditions

Basil seeds need a high and stable temperature to trigger germination. (20- 25°C). Once transplanted into the system, basil grows best in very hot conditions and in direct sunlight. However, a better quality of leaves is obtained with a minimum of shade. With daily temperatures above 27°C, plants should be ventilated or covered with a shade net of about 20%, especially during strong heat events and if solar radiation is excessive to avoid burns of the plant.

## Instructions

Transplant new plants into the system when they have 4-5 true leaves. Basil may be affected by a variety of fungal diseases, including fusarium, gray mold, and black spot. This occurs especially when temperatures fall below optimal thresholds and when humidity is high. Having an air and water temperature above 21°C night and day helps reduce plant stress and prevent the occurrence of disease.

## Harvesting

The harvest of the leaves begins when the plants reach 15 cm of height and continue for 30 to 50 days. Care should be taken when handling leaves at harvest time to prevent leaf bruising and blackening. It is advisable to remove flowering tops during the growth of the plant to avoid a bitter taste in the leaves and promote branching. However, basil flowers attract pollinators and beneficial insects.

Leaving a few flowering plants can improve the overall health of your garden and ensure a constant supply of basil seeds.

## Grow cauliflower in hydroponic

- Recommended ph: 6.0 to 6.5
- Plant spacing: 45-60 cm (3-5 plants/m 2)
- Germination time and temperature: 4-7 days with a temperature of 8 to 20 °C
- The growth time: 2-3 months (spring crops), 3-4 months (fall crops)
- Temperature r: ange20-25°C for initial vegetative growth, 10-15°C for head formation

Exposure to light: full sun

Height of the plant and width: 40-60 cm; 60-70 cm Recommended aquaponic method: culture beds

Cauliflower is a winter crop with high nutritional value that will grow and thrive in growth beds with proper plant spacing.

Cauliflower has a high nutrient demand, and plants respond positively to high levels of nitrogen and phosphorus.Among other nutrients, potassium and calcium are necessary for the production of buds.

The plant is sensitive to climatic conditions, and the heads do not grow properly when it is hot, very cold, or very dry. Therefore, the choice of varieties and the time allowed for transplanting are crucial.

## Growth conditions

The optimal air temperature for the initial vegetative growth of the plant is 15-25°C. For head formation, plants need cooler temperatures of 10-15°C for fall crops and 15-20°C for spring crops. It takes good humidity in the air, and that full sun conditions are met to develop good heads. Plants can tolerate cold temperatures. However, the heads can be damaged by frost. Light shade can be of benefit in warmer temperatures above 23°C.

## Instructions

Sprout the seeds in propagation tanks at 20-25°C. Provide direct sunlight from early planting stages so that the plants do not become "leggy".

When the plants are between 3 and 5 weeks old and 4 to 5 true leaves, you can start transplanting into the aquaponic system with a spacing of about 50 cm. To maintain the white color of the head, use strings of ropes or rubber to attach the leaves to the outside of the head when they are about 6-10 cm in diameter. Once this stage is reached, the harvest may take less than a week under ideal temperature conditions or one month under cooler conditions.

Excess sun, heat, or nitrogen absorption can cause the main flower to produce small grains of rice. Temperatures below 12°C could produce opposite buttons. The cauliflower is sensitive to certain pests like the flea beetle,

## Harvesting

The harvest is done when the heads are compact, white, and firm. Cut the heads with a large knife and remove the remaining plant and roots from the growing bed and place them in a compost bin.

## Grow lettuce in hydroponic

Lettuce plants have a shallow root system. They usually prefer smaller but more frequent irrigation sessions. During the hot summer months, we may need to water lettuce plants every day and possibly shade them.

If we do not water our plants regularly at this time of year, the lettuce plants suffer from heat and can shoot (the plant starts to produce seeds).

Consequently, lettuce leaves can become bitter. The shooting is generally irreversible, and these plants cannot be marketed. Most farmers use sprinkler or drip irrigation systems. To keep the soil consistently moist, farmers can apply a thin layer of mulch to the soil (ask a local expert).

It is strongly recommended to water lettuce early in the morning or late in the afternoon.

Excessive watering must be avoided, as this can lead to disease outbreaks and root rot. The moisture of the soil is the key to growing healthy salad.

## Seedling germination

1. Fill the plug trays with a moistened growing medium for grains. To make it wet, add water slowly and mix it with your hands until the medium is moist but not moist. Too much water can rot the seeds.

2. Sprinkle two to three lettuce seeds in each plug, cover them with ¼ inch moistened growing medium. Press lightly to establish a good ground-to-seed contact. Spray light or water to keep the soil moist during the germination period. For the best results, keep the soil at 60 to 68 degrees Fahrenheit.

3. Place the seedlings in a sunny location under fluorescent lighting as soon as they appear. Hold the lights about 2 centimeters above the plants and provide 14 hours of artificial light every day. Maintain an air temperature below 75 degrees f; lettuce is a cool crop. When the seedlings are about 2 centimeters long, thin for the strongest plant per plug.

## Instructions

Cut the four polystyrene panels with a kitchen knife, large them in a neat pile over the top of the shallow plastic container. Mark a polystyrene panel with guide marks for drilling the holes that contain the net pots. Use a highlighter and ruler to position the guide 12 inches apart, in staggered rows at a distance of 8 inches. Start 4 centimeters from the edge. A 2 by 4-foot panel usually contains 24 holes. Drilled the holes with a 2-inch hand saw drill, using the first panel as a template to make identical cuts in the remaining three polystyrene panels. Stack the four panels together and align the drill holes. Insert a net pot into each of the holes. Fill the plastic container with clean water. Allow about 2.5 cm of air between the top of the water and the bottom of the polystyrene panels so that the plants have access to oxygen. Thoroughly dissolve the ready-mix solution in the water. Rest the panels and pots on the plastic container. Remove the seedlings from the bins and carefully slide them into your palm one by one. Avoid pulling on the delicate stems - it can kill the plants. Slightly smooth the roots with your fingers and place a seedling in each net pot. Fold the carrots through the slats so that they dangle in the solution below. The seedlings are ready for the solution 2 to 3 weeks after planting in the dirt-free medium when they are approximately 2 centimeters long.

Place the plants under fluorescent light in a sunny location, with at least 14 hours of light per day. Regularly check the solution for signs of evaporation, replacing lost water to maintain the 1-inch air space. You do not have to add an additional solution. The time from germination to adulthood is typically five to six weeks. After harvesting, use the nutrient solution used to water other garden or house plants.

**Things you need**

- Plug trays (3/4 inch)
- Soilless growth medium
- Fluorescent lighting
- Polystyrene panels (1-inch thick)
- Knife
- Shallow plastic container, 4 to 6 inches deep
- Highlighter
- Ruler
- 2-inch hole saw drill
- Nutritional solution
- Water
- 2-inch net pots

**Tips**

Create your own net pots by cutting ½-inch slats into the sides of 2-inch plastic pots. Leave a 2-inch wide border close to the top to maintain structural integrity.

To prevent water fungus such as phytophthora or Pythium in your system, clean the drawer with bleach between crops. If your plants get infected, the crop is a loss.

Harvesting lettuce with attached roots extends shelf life by 2 to 4 weeks.

As an alternative to a ready-made solution, you make your own mixture. Add to 61 gallons of water, 180 grams of chem-gro, 108 grams of magnesium sulfate, and 180 gallons of calcium nitrate.

## Grow cucumbers in hydroponic

- Recommended ph: 5 to 6.5
- Plant spacing range: 30-60 cm (depending on variety, 2-5 plants/m 2)
- Germination time and temperature: 3-7 days; 20 to 30°C Growth time: 55-65 days
- Temperature: 22-28°C during the day, 18-20°C at night, susceptible to frost.
- Exposure to light: full sun
- Height of the plant and width: 20-200 cm; 20-80 cm
- Recommended aquaponic method: culture beds; dwc

Cucumbers are part of the Cucurbitaceae family (just like zucchini and melon) and are excellent summer fruits. These are ideal plants that thrive in growing beds because they have very large roots. Cucumber can also be grown on floating rafts, but there is a risk of clogging due to excessive root growth. Cucumbers require large amounts of nitrogen and potassium, and choosing these types of plants should be done with a good knowledge of the nutrients available in your system's water.

## Growing conditions

Cucumbers grow best on long, hot, humid days. They particularly like the hot nights. The optimal growth temperature is between 24 and 27 degrees during the day, with 70 to 90% humidity in the air.

The ideal substrate temperature is about 21°C. Plants stop growing at around 10-13°C. It is recommended to have a high concentration of potassium in order to promote the yield of cucumber better.

## Instructions

Cucumber plants can be transplanted from the age of 2-3 weeks, with four to five leaves. The plants grow very quickly, and it is interesting to limit the vigor of this plant that diverts nutrients when the stem is about 2 m long. It is necessary to remove the lateral branches, which favors the ventilation. The elongation of the plant is ensured by leaving only the two buttons furthest away from the main stem. Plants are encouraged to produce more. The presence of a pollinator is necessary for good fertilization and setting. Cucumber plants need support during growth and adequate ventilation to prevent foliar diseases such as powdery mildew and gray mold.

## Harvesting

Once transplanted, cucumbers can start production after 2-3 weeks. Under optimal conditions, the plants can be harvested 10-15 times. Collect every few days to prevent the fruits from becoming too important and to favor the growth of the following ones.

Grow eggplant in hydroponic

- Recommended ph: 5 to 7.0
- Plant spacing: 40-60 cm (3-5 plants/m 2)
- Germination time and temperature: 8-10 days; 25 to 30°C

Growth time: 90-120 days

- Temperature: 15-18°C at night, 22-26°C during the day; very sensitive to frost
- Exposure to light: full sun
- Height of the plant and width: 60-120 cm; 60-80 cm
- Recommended aquaponic method: culture beds

Eggplant is a summer-fruiting vegetable that grows well in substrate beds because of the deep growth of its root system.

Plants can produce 10 to 15 fruits for a total yield of 3 to 7 kg. Eggplants need a high nitrogen content and potassium requirements, which is important for the management choices of the number of plants to be grown in each aquaponic system to avoid a nutrient imbalance.

## Growing conditions

Eggplants love warm temperatures and full sun exposure. Eggplant plants have better yields with temperatures in the range of 22 to 26°C and ambient humidity of 60 to 70%. The fruit set is then favored. Temperatures below 10°C and above 32°C are very limiting.

## Instructions

Eggplant seeds germinate in 8 to 10 days at warm temperatures (26-30°C). The plants can be transplanted as soon as they have 4 to 5 leaves and when temperatures rise in the spring.

Towards the end of the summer season, starting a pinch of new flowers promotes the ripening of the existing fruit. At the end of the season, when bad weather arrives, the plants can be drastically pruned to 20-30 cm leaving only three branches.

This method interrupts the crop without killing the plants and allows the foot to spend the winter in expectation of the spring after. The plants can be grown without pruning.

However, in tight spaces or in greenhouses, branch management can be facilitated by stakes or vertical chains, especially if the weight of the fruit is too large.

In hot countries, eggplant is grown as a perennial. In France, it is grown as an annual.

## Harvesting

Eggplants are harvested when they are 10 to 15 cm long. The skin must be shiny. If it is dull and yellow, it is a sign that the fruit is too ripe. Delaying the harvest makes the fruits unmarketable due to the presence of seeds inside. Use a sharp knife and cut the eggplant off the plant leaving at least 3 cm of stem attached to the fruit.

## Grow peppers in hydroponic

- Recommended ph: 5 to 6.5
- Plant spacing: 30-60 cm (3-4 plants/m 2, or more for small varieties)
- Germination time and temperature: 8-12 days; 22 to 30°C (seeds will not germinate below 13°C)
- Growth time: 60-95 days
- Temperature: 14-16°C night, 22-30°C the day
- Exposure to light: full sun
- Height of the plant and width: 30-90 cm; 30-80 cm
- Recommended aquaponic method: culture beds

There are many varieties of peppers. But whether they are colorful for cooking or for the spicy sauce, they can all be grown in aquaponics. Peppers are more suitable for the culture bed method but can also be grown in 11 cm diameter nft tubes if they are given additional support with a tutor, for example.

## Growth conditions

Peppers have a summer fructification that prefers warm conditions and full sun exposure. Seed germination temperatures are high of the order of 22 to 34°C. Seeds do not germinate well at temperatures below 15°C. Daytime temperatures of 22 to 28°C and nocturnal temperatures of 14 to 16°C favor fruiting under better conditions at 60 to 65% ambient humidity. Optimum root temperatures are 15 to 20°C. In general, temperatures below 10-12°C stop the growth and give a deformation of the fruits, making them unsaleable. Temperatures above 30-35°C favor floral abortion. In general, spicy peppers (peppers) can be obtained at higher temperatures. The leaves of the top of the plant protect the fruit hanging under the sun.

As with other fruiting plants, the nitrates of the aquaponic system are sufficient for initial vegetative growth, but higher concentrations of potassium and phosphorus are required for flowering and fruiting.

## Instructions

Transplant seedlings with 6 to 8 true leaves as soon as night temperature does not drop below 10°C. Heavy plants should be helped and supported with stakes or vertical ropes suspended from horizontally drawn wire.

For red peppers, leave the green fruits on the plants until they ripen and turn red. Keep only the first flowers that appear on the plant to further encourage general growth. Reducing the number of flowers in the case of excessive fruiting will favor the growing fruits and allow them to reach a sufficient size quickly.

## Harvesting

Harvest peppers when they reach a marketable size. Leave the peppers on the plants until they ripen fully and change color by improving their vitamin c level. Gather continuously throughout the season to promote flowering, fruit set, and growth. Peppers can be easily stored for 10 days at 10°C with 90- 95% moisture, or they can be dehydrated for long-term storage.

## Grow tomatoes in hydroponic

- Recommended ph: 5.5 to 6.5
- Plant spacing: 40-60 cm (3-5 plants/m 2)
- Germination time and temperature: 4-6 days; 20 to 30°C
- Growth time: 50-70 days until the first harvest; fruiting 90-120 days up to 8-10 months (undetermined varieties)
- Optimum temperatures: 13-16°C night, day 22-26°C
- Exposure to light: full sun
- Height of the plant and width: 60-180 cm; 60-80 cm
- Recommended aquaponics method: culture beds and dwc

Tomatoes have excellent fruiting when grown in aquaponics, although physical support with stakes is required. Given the high nutrient demand of tomatoes, such as potassium, the number of plants per system must be planned according to the biomass of fish to avoid nutrient deficiencies. A high concentration of nitrogen is preferable from the first stages to promote the vegetative growth of plants. However, potassium should be supplied from the flowering stage to promote the fruiting of your tomatoes.

## Growth Conditions

Tomatoes prefer warm temperatures with full sun exposure. Below 8-10°C, plants stop growing, and nighttime temperatures range of 13-14°C to encourage fruit to set. Temperatures above 40°C cause poor fruit set. There are two types of tomato plants: determined (seasonal production) and indeterminate (continuous production of flower branches). For the first type, plants can be left as bushes leaving 3 to 4 main branches and removing all the greedy to divert the nutrients to the fruits. The two definite and indeterminate varieties must be grown with a single stem (double in case of high plant vigor) to remove all auxiliary (greedy) discards. However, in the varieties determined, only the apical point of the stem should be cut as soon as the plant reaches 7 to 8 floral branches to encourage fruiting. Tomatoes rest on supports that can be tied to vertical plastic/nylon ropes that are attached to horizontally drawn wire ropes over the system.

Tomatoes have a moderate tolerance to salinity like all Solanaceae. Higher salinity at the fruiting stage, however, improves the taste quality of the fruit.

Tomatoes rest on supports that can be tied to vertical plastic/nylon ropes that are attached to horizontally drawn wire ropes over the system. Tomatoes have a moderate tolerance to salinity like all Solanaceae. Higher salinity at the fruiting stage, however, improves the taste quality of the fruit. Tomatoes rest on supports that can be tied to vertical plastic/nylon ropes that are attached to horizontally drawn wire ropes over the system. Tomatoes have a moderate tolerance to salinity like all Solanaceae. Higher salinity at the fruiting stage, however, improves the taste quality of the fruit.

**Instructions**

Transplant 3-6 weeks after germination when seedling reaches 10-15 cm and when nighttime temperatures are consistently above 10°C. When transplanting plants, avoid waterlogging the roots to reduce the risk of disease. Once the tomato plants are up to 60 cm high, cut off unnecessary upper branches. Remove the bottom leaves 30 cm from the main stem to promote better air circulation and reduce fungal risk. Prune all auxiliary discards to promote fruit growth. Remove the leaves covering each branch of fruit soon before maturity to promote the flow of nutrition for fruits as well as exposure to the sun and accelerate ripening.

## Harvest

For better flavor, harvest the tomatoes when they are firm and have good color. The fruits will continue to mature if they are harvested at mid- maturity and brought indoors. The fruits can be stored for 2 to 4 weeks at 5-7°C under 85-90% relative humidity.

Grow beans and peas in hydroponic
- Recommended ph: 5 to 7.0
- Plant spacing: 10-30 cm depending on the variety (bush varieties 20-40 plants/m 2, climbing plant varieties 10-12/m 2)
- Germination time and temperature: 8-10 days; 21 to 26°C
- Growth time: 50-110 days to reach maturity depending on the variety
- Temperature: 16-18°C night, day 22-26°C
- Exposure to light: full sun
- Height of the plant and width: 60-250 cm (climbers); 60-80 cm (dwarf beans)
- Recommended aquaponic method: culture bed

Climbing beans and kidney beans grow very well in aquaponics, but the first ones are recommended to optimize the space of a bed of culture. The climbing varieties allow two to three times more harvest than the kidney beans. Beans have low nitrate requirements but a moderate demand in terms of phosphorus and potassium.

These nutrient requirements make beans an ideal choice for aquaponic production, although excess nitrate may delay flowering. Beans are recommended on a new aquaponic system as they can fix atmospheric nitrogen.

## Growing conditions

Climbing varieties enjoy full sun but tolerate partial shade under high- temperature conditions. Plants do not grow at temperatures below 12°C and above 35°C, temperatures cause floral abortion and fruit set. The optimum moisture content for plants is 70-80%. Beans are sensitive to the photoperiod, so it is important to choose the right varieties according to geographical location and season.

In general, climbing varieties are grown in summer, while dwarf varieties are adapted to the short-day conditions of spring and fall.

## Instructions

For bedded systems, seed should be placed directly in the bed 3 to 4 cm deep, ensuring that the bell siphon allows a sufficiently high water level during germination. Beans do not burrow well, which makes them difficult to grow in a nft.

All supporting poles should be placed before seed germination to prevent root damage. In sowing, precautions must be taken to avoid any interaction with other plants.

Beans are susceptible to aphids and mites. You will have to pay close attention to the choice of companion plants of your beans to avoid contamination.

## Harvesting

Varieties of green beans (green or yellow wax beans): the pods must be firm and crunchy at harvest time. The seeds must be small inside. Immobilize the stem with one hand and harvest with the other to avoid pulling branches that will allow subsequent picking. Remove all ripe pods to keep the plants productive.

Shell beans: harvest these varieties when there is a color change on the pods, and the beans are fully formed inside but not dried. The pods should be plump and firm. Their quality declines if they are left on the plant too long.

Dry beans (beans and soybeans): when the pods become as dry as possible and before a weather refresh or when the plants have turned brown and lost most of their leaves. The pods can easily split.

## Grow cabbage in hydroponic

- Recommended ph: 6 to 7.2
- Plant spacing: 60-80 cm (4-8 plants/m 2)
- Germination time and temperature: 4-7 days; 8 to 29°C
- Growth time: 45-70 days from transplant (depending on variety and season)

- Ideal temperature: 15-20°C (growth stops above 25°C)
- Exposure to light: full sun
- Height of the plant and width: 30-60 cm; 30-60 cm
- Recommended aquaponics method: culture beds (not suitable for aquaponic systems receiving)

Grow cabbage in aquaponics: cabbage is grown in winter and grows best in a growing bed because it reaches important dimensions at harvest and therefore is too big and too heavy for growing in raft or nft. Cabbage is a nutrient-demanding plant that makes it incompatible with aquaponics systems that are less than four months old. Nevertheless, because of the large space required, cabbage crops take fewer nutrients per square meter than other fall and winter leafy vegetables such as lettuce, spinach, rocket, etc. Cabbage can tolerate low temperatures, such as 5°C.

**Growing conditions**

The cabbage is suitable for fall and winter crops with ideal growth temperatures between 15 and 20°C. Cabbage grows best when the heads are in cooler temperatures. It is advisable to plan to harvest before daytime temperatures reach 23 to 25°C.

High concentrations of phosphorus and potassium are essential when the buds begin to grow.

## Instructions

Young plants must be transplanted when they have 4 to 6 leaves and a height of 15 cm.

Cabbage needs an optimal planting density depending on the variety chosen. In case the daytime temperature is above 25°C, use a shade net with a 20% filter to prevent bolting of the plant, which will prevent it from going to seed. Given the high incidence of cabbage worms and other pests such as aphids, root maggots, and cabbage looper, careful monitoring is important.

## Harvesting

Start harvesting when the cabbage heads are firm with a diameter of about 10 to 15 cm depending on the varieties grown. Cut the head of the stem with a large knife and place the outer leaves in the compost bin. If cabbage heads tend to break, this indicates that they are too ripe and should have been harvested earlier.

## Grow broccoli in hydroponic

- Recommended ph: 6 to 7
- Plant spacing: 40-70 cm (3-5 plants/m 2)
- Germination time and temperature: 4-6 days at 25°C minimum
- Growth time: 60-100 days from transplanting
- Average daily temperature: 13-18°C
- Exposure to light: full sun but can tolerate partial shade

- Height of the plant and width: 30-60 cm; 30-60 cm
- Recommended aquaponic method: culture beds

Broccoli is a nutritious vegetable of autumn and winter. We recommend growing it in a bed of culture because broccoli is a bulky and heavy plant at harvest. Broccoli is moderately hard to grow, but it is a nutrient demanding plant. It is also very sensitive to high temperatures. You must select the variety to grow based on your geographic location and climate. Broccoli grows best when the daytime temperatures are between 14 and 17°C.

For the formation of the head, the various varieties require temperatures ranging between 10 and 15°C. It accepts higher temperatures provided that the rate of humidity is higher. Hot temperatures can cause premature bolting.

## Instructions

Young plants in beds should be transplanted when they have 4 to 5 true leaves, and the plants reach 15 to 20 cm high.

Plants should be spaced from 40 to 50 cm apart as closer spacing will result in smaller central heads.

Broccoli and cabbage are vulnerable to cabbage worms and other persistent parasites, so be careful.

## Harvesting

For best quality, start harvesting broccoli when buds in the head are firm and tight. Harvest as soon as possible if the buds start to separate and flower starts (yellow flowers).

## Grow swiss chard and beetroot in hydroponic

- Recommended ph: 6 to 7.5
- Plant spacing: 30-30 cm (15-20 plants/m 2)
- Germination time and temperature: 4-5 days; 25 to 30°C (preferably 30 °)
- Growth time: 25-35 days
- Temperature: 16-24°C
- Exposure to light: full sun (partial shade for temperatures above 26°C)
- Height of the plant and width: 30-60 cm; 30-40 cm
- Recommended aquaponics method: culture beds, nft and dwc pipes

Swiss chard is an extremely popular green vegetable in aquaponics that can be grown easily.

It is a low nitrate vegetable that requires lower potassium and phosphorus levels than other fruits and vegetables, making it an ideal plant for aquaponics in a young aquaponic system.

Due to its high market value, rapid growth rate, and nutritional content, swiss chard are frequently grown in commercial aquaponics systems. Its foliage is dark green, but the stems can have striking and attractive colors like yellow, purple, or red.

## Growing conditions

Optimum temperatures are 16 to 24°C, while the minimum growth temperature is 5°C. Although traditionally a moderate jelly tolerant crop, swiss chard can grow as well in the open sun during the mild summer seasons.

A shade net is suggested at higher temperatures. Swiss chard has a minimal tolerance to salinity. Swiss chard seeds produce more than one seedling, so thinning is needed as soon as the seedling starts to sprout.

As plants become senescent during the season, old leaves can be removed to encourage new growth.

## Harvesting

Swiss chard leaves can be cut permanently when they reach exploitable sizes. The elimination of large leaves promotes the growth of news. Avoid damaging the growth point in the center of the plant at harvest.

## Grow parsley in hydroponic

- Recommended ph: 6 to 7
- Plant spacing: 15-30 cm (10-15 plants/m 2)
- Germination time and temperature: 8-10 days; 20 to 25°C
- Growth time: 20-30 days after transplantation Temperature: 15-25°C
- Exposure to light: full sun; partial shade at> 25°C
- Height of the plant and width: 30-60 cm; 30-40 cm
- Recommended aquaponics method: culture beds, nft and dwc

Parsley is a plant very commonly grown in commercial aquaponic systems because of its nutritional content. Indeed, parsley is rich in vitamins a and c, calcium, and iron. It has a high market value and is an easy plant to grow with relatively low nutrient requirements compared to other vegetables.

## Growing conditions

Parsley is a bi-annual plant, but it is traditionally grown as an annual. Larger varieties will grow over a two year period if the winter season is mild with minimal frost. Although the plant can withstand temperatures of 0°C, the minimum temperature for its growth is 8°C. In the first year, the plants produce leaves, while in the second, the plants begin to develop flower stems for seed production.

Parsley gets all the benefits of the full sun by being exposed up to eight hours a day. However, partial shading is required for temperatures above 25°C.

## Instructions

The main difficulty when parsley grows is the initial germination that can take between two and five weeks, depending on the freshness of the seeds. To hasting germination, the seeds can be soaked in hot water at about 20-23°C for 24-48 hours to soften the seed coat. Then empty the water and sow the seeds in germinating trays. Emerging seedlings will look like grass with two narrow, opposite leaves. After 5 to 6 weeks, transplant the plants into the aquaponic system in early spring.

## Harvesting

Start harvesting once the individual stems of the plant reach at least 15 cm long. Harvesting the first shoots of the plant will encourage growth throughout the season.

If the best leaves are cut, the plant will remain less productive. If the parsley has dried, it can be crushed with the hand and stored in an airtight container.

## Basic overview of the cultivation of cannabis

Whether you choose the more popular sativa for a high or Indica for its soothing and healing effects, most of the growth process is the same. You can cut the top of an Indica to give it more shrubbery, but the way you pour and feed both types of plants is the same.

First, check the temperature in the breeding room. The best range for cannabis is 28-30 °C, but not more than 30 degrees. With hydroponics, one also usually has to keep an eye on the temperature of the water in the system. The ideal temperature is between 17 and 22 degrees. This ensures maximum nutrient uptake and sufficient dissolved oxygen levels to keep the roots healthy and rot-free.

Second, use filtered or pure well water to avoid the supply of chlorine and fluoride. After adding the nutrients to the water, check the ph to make sure the solution is slightly acidic, between 5.5 and 6.5, with 6.15 being about right.

Third, follow the guidance of the light. Hang the light at the correct distance from the tops of the plants and make sure that the light reaches the edges of the crop. Here a growth tent lined with mylar helps to reflect the light onto the plants.

Run the light for the required time according to the growth phase of the plant. You do not need light to germinate. Once you have sprouted, you can let the light run for 18 hours a day until you reach half of its final height (which depends on the load on the grass). To bloom, it only takes 12 hours of light per day.

One or two weeks after flowering, it's time to separate males and females. You do not want them to multiply if you do not try to get seeds. Females get white hair and male balls. Yes, balls. You cannot smoke balls, so you get rid of them. They are only good for pollen.

About two weeks before the harvest, you leave the nutrients away and give the plants only water. This reduces the nutrient content. When harvesting the plants, you cut with a bud trimmer or by hand the plants and dry them. Store them in an airtight container for two weeks to a month to allow them to set.

Now that we've talked about the primary way to grow cannabis, let's take a look at the types of hydroponic systems, how they work, and what the pros and cons they have.

**JAMIE BACKYARD**

# Chapter 4:
# Common Problems

Because hydroponic plants can be completely sealed off from the environment by installation in greenhouses, problems with plant pests are much lower than in conventional fields. However, other difficulties arise: due to the often warm temperatures in the greenhouses and (especially with the dripping method) many thin lines, the water heats up quickly. This reduces the possibility of binding oxygen and co2. Biofilms are another problem—slimy forms of algae, protozoa, and fungi that form quite quickly. These plaques can clog parts of the irrigation system, causing crop failures. Besides, biofilms are an excellent reservoir for bacteria and fungi that can damage the roots of plants.

## Algae in hydroponic

Algae can be a problem in any type of hydroponics. In a bubbler system, it often takes place in the nutrient reservoir, especially when the container lets in light.

Building up algae reduces the nutrients in the system, which makes the plants work harder as they compete with the algae for food.

Algae can also coat the airstone, which is the part of the system that creates the bubbles.

The thicker the algae become, the more difficult it is for bubbles to escape, resulting in reduced oxygenation of the water.

## Possible diseases and pests in indoor plants

Houseplants with hard leaves are less susceptible to pests, as they cannot easily grip the leaf.

Therefore, it is particularly effective in these plants to spray the plant simply with a hard water-steel. In plants such as a sansevieria or the chamaerops humilis, you can occasionally inject with a pressure sprayer now and then as a preventative measure.

Specific information on certain pests, vermin species, diseases, or pests can be found here:

- Spider mites
- Scale lice
- Wolllaus

## Spider mites

Spider mites are an infection of mites on the plant. Characteristic of the spinnmilde is the small, pear-shaped body, which is about as big as a pinhead.

If plants are affected by spider mites, they are deprived of the necessary nutrients.

## Variants of the pest

Spider mites are available in many different variations, most of which are plant-specific. For example, the common spider mite is common in greenhouses.

## Susceptible plants

Depending on the spider mite species, other plants are susceptible. Examples of susceptible plants are the alocasia and the polyscias. Above all, however, plants that are often in dry soil are the most susceptible to an infection of spider mites.

## Place of infestation

The spider mites often sit under the leaves. Since they are very small and move little, but they are difficult to discover.

## Appearance

The spider mites are about 0.3 and 0.5mm in size and have a pear-shaped body. Depending on the species, spider mites have a brown, red or yellow- green color. The best way to recognize a spider mite infestation on the leaves of plants. Because these get brown, almost coppery points and after a while yellow or brown and fall off. In the case of a longer infestation, a white tissue often appears on the underside of the leaves.

## Reason

Like other mite species, spider mites also become active in warm and dry weather. Often spider mites also occur through old soil. Because of the earth no longer has any nutrients, this is the perfect place for the spider mite to develop. Since even weak plants are frequently attacked, it often helps to repot the plant and thereby give it energy and resistance again.

## Distribution

Spider mites benefit from their size and agility. This allows spider mites to reproduce easily through plant-to-plant contact.

## Damage to the plant

Spider mites poke small holes in the leaves, sucking nutrients out of the plant. As a result, the plant can no longer transport or absorb nutrients and will most likely die from prolonged infestation. If the spider mite is not fought well and on time, it becomes a pretty stubborn plague for any plant.

## Fighting

Prevention is easier than getting rid of it. Therefore, we recommend occasionally spraying your plants with pesticides. You can also prevent infestation by spraying with water, as spider mites prefer a dry environment. There are several ways to fight spider mites. First of all, we recommend removing the affected leaves and branches. Do not try to touch the healthy branches with the affected branches. In case of heavy infestation, it is best to use a control agent. The spider mite, in contrast to various louse species, has little resistance to preservatives. Particularly difficult in combating the spider mite is the size of these parasites.

These are easy to miss and can then easily spread again. Therefore, the plant should be sprayed thoroughly. Tip: in the evening, spray the plant with water containing 2% yellow soap and 1% spirit. Since the eggs hatch mostly in the evening, this is particularly effective. In addition, you can increase humidity and reduce temperature. Because spider mites love a warm, dry environment.

## Harmfulness to humans
For humans, spider mites are not dangerous.

## Special features
At a temperature of below 12 degrees, spider mites stop evolving and go into their rest period.

## Scale lice
Scale lice are often confused with lice. They have an eponymous flat body and are represented in various colors. Scale insects are difficult to control and can cause great damage to the plant.

## Variants of the pest

There are two types of scale insects. The boisdubal schildlaus are flat, yellow lice, in which the male are smaller than the female.

These are often confused with lice (lice), the lice have a rectangular body. The second species is the oleander schildlaus.

These have an eponymous round shield, which, however, is not in the middle. Due to the color (white or yellow), and the shape of the 2mm pests is often compared with fried eggs.

## Susceptible plants

Thyme louse occurs most often in older plants or plants with a woody stem. It is also common in orchids and all types of palm trees.

place of infestation:

Both types of scale lice occur on the underside of the leaves as well as in the trunk.

## Appearance

In most cases, scale insects live in a group, which together forms a thick crust.

Since the male scale insects have a waxy powder, they are often mistaken for woolly lice.

Scale insects occur in different colors, including white, gray, or yellow.

## Reason

Often the scale louse occurs in a dry air environment. In addition, an abundance of lime in the soil or a poorly-groomed plant may be a cause of scale insects.

## Distribution

Scale insects spread through insects, birds, or the wind. In indoor plants, they spread by drafts, pets, or contact with clothes.

## Damage to the plant

The insect lice attach to the plant and inject a toxic substance into the cells. This substance causes yellow, brown, or red spots on the leaves or flowers. If the pest is not fought, this leads to permanent malformation or even death of the plant.

## Fighting

The louse is difficult to fight. Most of the time, there is no alternative but to use chemical means to control. If you do not want to use chemistry, you can also tap the lice with a cotton bud soaked in olive oil. The oil closes the breathing tube of the louse, and the louse will suffocate. Preventive treatment with chemical agents is effective only with repeated use. After contact with scale insects, wash and disinfect your hands carefully to avoid spreading through eggs.

## Harmfulness to humans

Scale insects are not harmful to humans.

## Special features

Scale lice form their shield by separating the substance itself. This shield is hard on the outside and soft on the inside. The scale insects are between 1 and 3 mm in size and lay about 100 eggs. While male scale insects only live for a maximum of 2 days, female scale insects can live up to 120 days. The scale insects are among the few species that can reproduce both sexually and asexually.

## Wolllaus

The wolllaus belongs to the family of the louse (pseudococcidae). The name is the typical greasy hairiness of these lice. If it is not treated in time, the lice may spread to all plants.

## Variants of the pest

There are several types of lice, of which the citrus louse (planococcus citri) is best known. She lives about 40 days with a heat of about 22°C. She is the only species that reproduce sexually. The louse lays in about 100 eggs, which hatch after 2 weeks.

Another common species is the long-tailed louse (pseudococcus longispinus). This louse occurs mainly in a humid environment.

## Susceptible plants

Woll lice can be found on all indoor plants. However, houseplants such as the more vulnerable are the pineapple, orchid, cactus, passionflower, bromeliad, olive tree, crassula species, and the musa (banana plant) as other species.

## Place of infestation

Where exactly lice attack the plant depends on the type of lice. While most lice nest directly on the plant, some species feed on the roots. The wolllaus is one of the few plagues in the world. In the summer months, the birds louse up to 100 eggs, which then hatch within 2 weeks.

## Appearance

The lice have a size of 3 to 6 mm and are covered with white, floury discharge from wax wires. They use this layer to protect themselves from the elements and natural enemies. In addition, lay your eggs in this layer.

## Reason

Although plants in drafts are more susceptible to woolly louse infestations, the mealybugs have no special requirements for a plant to infect them.

## Distribution

Woll lice live in large groups, but they do not spread themselves, but are mostly the people responsible for the distribution over the clothes.

## Damage to the plant

The mealybugs feed on phloem. This is the system that provides the plants with nutrients. The lice with their mouthparts suck the phloem out of the leaves, which causes the plant to lose waxing power. In addition, the plant can thereby get yellow or brown leaves and even must be educated. In addition, the hunts honeydew off, which is an optimal place for the formation of shimmer. As the honeydew mixes with the wool-like secretion, the leaf is completely covered. As a result, the plant receives less light, and photosynthesis becomes more difficult.

## Fighting

Woll lice are cold-resistant. They can even easily survive temperatures of minus 40 degrees. For the fight, you can mix 12 grams of paraffin oil to one liter of water and spray over the lice. Alternatively, you can do this with alcohol.

You must repeat this treatment thoroughly each day to be sure that the fluid has touched all lice. You can also use a pressure sprayer to simply rinse away the lice. In the case of long-term infestation, however, we recommend using chemical control.

## Harmfulness to humans
Mealybugs are not harmful to humans.

## Special features
Most mealybugs can reproduce both sexually and asexually.

## Wool and lice
In dry room air, wool and mealybugs can spread undisturbed:
- Infestation leaves a wooly coating on the stems and leaves
- Oil-containing sprays help, for example with neem oil
- The oil stifles the lice

## Black or green lice
The cause of an infestation with black or green lice is often too dry and warm location, especially places above a radiator and in the blazing sun:
- Makes visible by curling the leaves
- Especially young shoots take damage
- Formation of a sticky coating
- Wash off lice with a detergent-based solution
- Change location

## Schildlaus

Similar to the other lice, too dry air promotes the spread of scale insects:

- Brown cusps on the stems and leaves
- Glued leaves that lead to crippling
- Oil-containing sprays are also used here

## Healing of infested plants

To slow the spread of the pests, remove as much infected material as possible. Either cut away the infested material completely, or you try to remove the pests with a cloth. After you have come into contact with the vermin, you should disinfect your hands.

Place the plant outside or cover the floor with foils so you can "shower" it off with lukewarm water. This also works preventively. You can use a hard jet of water to simply rinse away most of the plague.

If your infested houseplant is also suitable for outdoors, you can also put it outside to prevent infection of other plants. For example, you can fight the spider mite completely. Make sure, however, that the outside temperature is high enough, and the plant is not in direct sunlight.

If you want to combat the pests with chemicals, multiple treatments are necessary. Therefore, pay close attention to the enclosed instructions for your particular product.

After successful treatment, spray the plant with lukewarm rainwater to rinse off the remainder of the chemicals.

Also, clean the planter completely. Take the plant completely out of the pot and remove as much old soil as possible. In addition, check the roots of the plant for your health. Then you can refill the plant pot with new soil.

**Causes**

Particularly susceptible to vermin, houseplants are not properly maintained or permanently draughty. For example, if a plant has a lack of water, it can make the leaves softer, making it easier for lice to extract the juice from the plant. Of course, healthy plants can also be attacked by pests. These can often spread unnoticed by pets, other plants, or even by yourself first. Therefore, it is important to regularly check your plants for pests, paying particular attention to the lower side of the leaves. Because if you see something that does not belong there, you may be able to save the plant in time. If lice or spider mites completely attack your plant, it will be difficult for your plant.

**JAMIE BACKYARD**

# Chapter 5:
# Tips for Growing Healthy Plants

Use these tips from experts to help you get started in hydroponics.

- Water the plants every few days when they are new, then water them once a day when they are blooming.
- Use a hygrometer to check the moisture content or water when the top of the potting substrate feels dry.
- Watch the leaves to see if they are withering or hanging - these are signs of too much or too little water.
- When plants bloom, some leaves may turn yellow and fall off. Stop giving nutrients, just water, because, in a week or two, you will reap.
- Harvest when half or three-quarters of the white hair has turned yellow-brown, and the trichomes have turned white or yellowish.
- Late harvesting provides more "relaxing" marijuana.
- You can tell when buds are dry enough when they tear off clean, instead of bending.

## How do you test the ph?

- The right amount of acid is essential for the cultivation of healthy cannabis. The right ph means that the nutrients are properly absorbed. Here is a brief overview of how to test ph values.

- The ph of the soil ranges from 1 to 14, with 1 very acid and 14 very alkaline and 7 neutral.

- The ideal for hydroponically grown grass is 5.5 to 6.5, just slightly sour. (in normal soil, you should be between 6.0 and 7.0) you can test the values in two places - the nutrient solution itself and the "soil" on which the plants grow.

Use a test pen, strip, or liquid solution to get results.

Take samples of nutrient solution or soil and use the tester to see how high the acidity is.

## How to set acidic or alkaline ph values?

Do not panic if your level varies a bit from day to day. The grass can handle it. But if you go below 5.5 or above 6.5, you can quickly face danger.

It's best to get the levels back up as fast as possible. For control, several easy-to-use ph control kits contain a ph tester.

Some experienced breeders know how to correct the ph level with household items such as baking soda and vinegar, but we do not recommend this for newcomers.

## How to stop root rot

Root rot hides from our eyes and remains undetected for so long. When the first visible clues show on the plant, her health is almost ruined. Now it is time to act quickly.

## Safely detect root rot

Recognizing rotting roots is not easy because they are invisible to us, surrounded by the earth. But at some point, this disease cannot be overlooked on the rest of the plant. The typical picture shows a wilting plant. The plant needs water, thinks the owner, and pours vigorously. The rot remains undiscovered, even more, advanced with more wetness. When wilting parts of plants or changes in the leaves, root rot should always be considered:

- Dig out and inspect roots
- Look for a gray, brown or black discoloration
- Rotten roots are often mushy
- They spread a musty smell
- Immediate measures

Root rot often means the end of the plant, but sometimes the salvation can succeed.

The effective preparation is not available on the market, especially as different pathogens are at work.

Since wet soil contributes significantly to the onset and progression of the disease, here lies the key:

Cut off foul roots completely

Rinse root bales under running water Plant in fresh soil

Use a new pot.

## Tips

In the following period, keep the plant mostly dry so that their roots can recover.

- Root rot in the garden bed: if whole vegetable beds or certain plants in the open are affected by the root rot, the rescue becomes more difficult. First of all, casting behavior is put to the test. Depending on the root disease, it may also be necessary to dispose of affected plants immediately and completely. Nevertheless, some pathogens survive in the soil and often infest the same plant species. Therefore, pay attention to the crop rotation in the following years.
- Prevent root rot: even if the infected plant dies of root rot, it is high time for preventive measures. For other plants and new acquisitions, there is also the risk of developing root rot during their lifetime. At least care mistakes as risk factors should be minimized.
- Avoid waterlogging/empty coasters
- Use a loose, well-drained substrate
- Use plant tonic
- Always observe crop rotation in the bed.

# Conclusion

Hydroponics is an economical, environmentally friendly way to grow plants and produce without soil or pesticides. The plants grow faster and produce bigger yields while being completely GMO-free, making them a lot healthier to eat.

Not only does hydroponics allow for fast, efficient, cost effective growing environments, but it is a means to grow produce where it otherwise was not able to grow. Thanks to innovative irrigation systems and the use of various growing media, places that have inadequate soil composition are able to grow fresh produce.

Hydroponics also provides a growing solution for places that have little to no space for commercial growing lands. It has even been successfully tested in space. Hydroponics is not a new concept but has come a long way since ancient times and keeps moving forward in leaps and bounds with new methods being introduced along the way.

It is not a hard concept to grasp and some methods are really easy to learn. There are ready-made kits that one can buy and assemble for each type of system. But they are all capable of being homemade with materials found around the home.

Hydroponics is a great way to teach children the joy of gardening without the mess of dirt and as the plants grow relatively quickly it holds their attention better than normal gardening does.

There are many exciting growing opportunities to be had with hydroponics and if done right, you will be rewarded with bountiful, healthy crops.

Aquaponics adds another dynamic level to the sustainable green farming in that it utilizes natural nutrients generated from a fish tank to organically nourish a media bed. In turn, the media beds offer the fish tank clean water as they filter out all the waste products and return clean water to the fish tank.

**JAMIE BACKYARD**

# Hydroponics

A Step-By-Step Guide to Grow Plants in Your Greenhouse Garden. Discover the Secrets of Hydroponics and Build an Inexpensive System at Home for Growing Herbs and Vegetables All-Year-Round

By:
## Jamie Backyard

**JAMIE BACKYARD**

# TABLE OF CONTENTS

Introduction ............................................................................ 230

Chapter 1: What is Hydroponics? ................................... 232

Chapter 2: Types Of Hydroponic Systems .................... 244

Chapter 3: Hydroponics Growing Medium ................... 272

Chapter 4: Lightning ......................................................... 310

Chapter 5: Guide To Create Your Own Hydroponic System ............................................................................................. 324

Chapter 6: Plant Nutrition ............................................... 328

Conclusion ......................................................................... 336

**JAMIE BACKYARD**

# Introduction

**H**ydroponics is the science of water, and when we talk about hydroponics, it's simply about hydroponics linked to plants. The hydrofoils are without exception all very shapely; they have an insert that consists of a grid. An important part is gravel. He should hold the plant from the roots to the edge of the pot, but let air and oxygen through. Basalt gravel has proven to be best because it is lime-free. The most important, however, is the nutrient salt, because the water alone cannot naturally feed a plant. Here we take the plant nutrient salt "we pot them and rinse their root ball in warm water until the very last soil between the fine rootlets has disappeared. The root system must be completely clean. Then we take the use of the hydraulic vessel and scatter coarse gravel on the grid so that no stones can slip through. Then the plant comes in and is filled up with the finer gravel to the edge. In the hydrolase, we solve that "hydral" on, always in the ratio of 1 gram of nutrient salt to 1 liter of water. The water level must only reach the marking groove so that there is still air between the application soil and the water level, and the plant gets oxygen.

# Chapter 1:
# What is Hydroponics?

Hydroponic plant breeding is seen as a future problem solver for the global food crisis caused by the increasing world population and climate change. Hydroculture is nothing more than plants without soil. The plants grow exclusively in expanded clay. These are these globules that are created by burning the clay at 1200 degrees and then bloating it. Expanded clay does not store water or nutrients. Inside are only air and sound. The plants grow from the beginning in expanded clay. Although it is possible to transplant soil plants into hydroponic plants, it is usually not practicable because the plants need a long time to get used to, and success is not guaranteed. Hydroculture means that the plant wholly cleaned from the soil is planted in a watertight vessel having a water level indicator with a substrate such as expanded clay. The watertight vessel is necessary because the whole time, there is water with a nutrient solution for the plants in the pot, about which the water level indicator permanently provides information. The most common substrate is currently expanded clay beads made from baked clay. These are also known under the brand name "lecaton" but other substrates, such as perlite, basalt, mineral wool, gravel, sand, and also polystyrene flakes are suitable for hydroponics. Soilless cultivation of plants in inorganic substrates is known to many hobby gardeners.

Hydroculture is the broader sense, which means that plants are cultivated in the water. However, more narrowly stated, it is a system that allows plant growth without the use of potting soil or soil. Hydroculture is very popular amongst private gardeners because of the many benefits it offers. Especially with plant friends who manage in a small space or without a garden, perfect results can be achieved with hydroponics. Typical advantages of hydroponic culture are that no weeds have to be removed, no pests in the soil have to be combated, and that the sensitivity to stress and thus diseases are often reduced. Therefore, plants that grow in hydroponic plants are healthier, grow faster, and flower more quickly, and eventually produce fruit. Another advantage is that through specific extensions, a hydroponic system can also be supplied semi-automatically or fully automatically with water and nutrients. It is therefore also suitable for those The care of the original hydroponic culture is facilitated conditionally by the system. The water level gauge usually has three levels, minimum, optimum, and maximum, to ensure optimal, plant-specific care. Of course, as in normal houseplants, the watering intervals of hydro plants vary depending on the pitch, the pot size, and the plant itself. The cleaning of plants, removing dead leaves or parts of plants, and the regular pruning and control of animal and fungal infestation should be regular, respectively.

## What plants need to grow ?

Plants can evidently build up almost out of nowhere. A bit of water, light, air, and earth seem to be enough to make a small seed to grow a whole shrub. Using carbon from the air, they use the sun's energy to make glucose, which they use to fuel their growth and cell buildup. In fact, plants are so-called autotrophic organisms, i.e. They produce their own food. Of course, they cannot arise out of anywhere. Complex conditions and their precise coordination are necessary to guarantee stable, healthy growth.

## Light:

Light could almost be described as the most crucial growth factor. It splits the water molecules so that the further process can be triggered, and photosynthesis is started. Too little light leads to the so-called geilwuchs, whereby root development and leaf growth are neglected in favor of the growth of length so that the plant can get better at a light source. This makes sense when other larger plants cover the smaller one.

However, if there is too little light at all, for example, in the interior, the plant can logically still be so long and will not get a photon.

In addition, one can observe in plant growth that they always stretch to the sun. The shadow side of a plant grows faster and faster, so that it inclines towards the sun, to get a maximum of radiation. But not only the direction, but also the nature of the light changes the growth of the plant.

Depending on the intensity and wavelengths, different substances form, or the plant generally grows more or less well.

To ensure this environmental factor, you can use artificial light in the form of led plant light, which covers all the wavelengths required for growth and promise better results than purely monochrome light.

## Air:

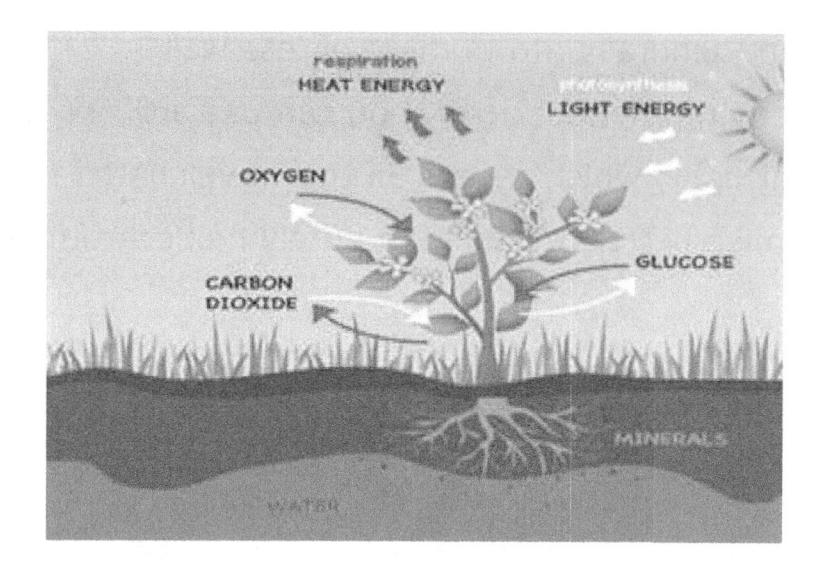

The carbon dioxide that the plant needs for its construction, it gets from the air. There plant finds, namely, aside from all other gases, carbon dioxide (co2).

Inorganic co2 is used to produce important organic compounds that act as building material and energy sources for different parts of the ecosystem. For example, our vegetable diet serves us as an energy source because the plants process the carbon from the air.

## Minerals, nitrogen and other nutrients

The nutrient solution in the hydroponic system is probably the most important factor for success or failure. Unlike fertilizers for garden soils or potting soil, hydroponics requires all nutrient elements. In addition to the known primary nutrients nitrogen, phosphorus, and potassium, these also include magnesium, iron, and trace nutrients such as boron, manganese, and zinc. In addition to the usual liquid fertilizers, various long-term fertilizers are available, which ensure the supply for up to four months. Commercially available fertilizers, which are often cheaper than pure hydroponic fertilizers, also work well. However, the user should be experienced in handling fertilizers. The result of wrong feeding can be salinisation or overdosage.

Having arrived at the nutrients the plant needs for healthy growth, we enter into phytotrophology. A complex term that, in principle, means nothing other than the nutritional science of the plant (phyton means plant and trophology means nutrition). In principle, plants are autotrophic organisms. They can virtually produce their own food. They do this in photosynthesis, where they produce glucose and oxygen from carbon dioxide and water by supplying energy in the form of light.

With this glucose, they get their processes going so that cells can be built up. They also need nutrients from the soil that they absorb through the roots.

These include the following substances:

- Nitrogen
- Phosphate
- Potassium
- Calcium
- Sulfur
- Magnesium

## The pros and cons

Hydroculture has some advantages, especially for those who forget to plant their plants quickly.

But you should know their disadvantages before you decide for or against the hydroponic culture. In the following some important points will be showed.

## Advantages of hydroponic culture

Hydroponic plants are very easy to care for and can be left alone for a while.

This is especially beneficial for people who are often traveling or for other reasons, and cannot take care of their plants regularly.

The right watering is easy with the hydroponics, because with them the water level indicator shows, whether water has to be refilled again. In the case of plants in soil, however, it happens so quickly that they are poured too much or too little. Even a sufficient supply of nutrients is easier in the hydroponic culture than in the culture in soil. With it, the fertilizer can be precisely metered.

The fertilization can be done either by a liquid fertilizer or a long-term fertilizer. For the roots of plants, the air is just as important as sufficient water and nutrients. Between the beads of expanded clay, they get this air much easier than in potting soil, which often condenses with time.

Allergy sufferers, asthmatics, and other sensitive persons benefit from the fact that hardly any allergenic substances such as fungal spores are released into the air during hydroponic cultivation. However, to take advantage of this, it is important to clean the expanded clay periodically. Pests that live in soil find no breeding ground. Plants are more durable than soil cultures - which offers a cost advantage and, in addition to all the numerous benefits of hydroponics, justifies the slightly higher price.

If vessels and substrates are cleaned regularly, the hydroponic culture itself is suitable for hospitals, nursing homes, and other facilities in which hygiene plays an extremely important role. Repotting is less required in hydroponics than in plants in soil.

New pots, buckets or trays must therefore usually be bought only after a few years. Besides, repotting is associated with less dirt.

## Disadvantages of hydroponic culture

For hydroponic cultivation, only special planters are suitable, which are waterproof and ideally already equipped with a water level indicator and a shaft for the fertilizer. They are often more expensive than traditional flowerpots.

The substrate, the pot, and the water level indicator should be cleaned once a year, although this work is not difficult, with a corresponding number of plants but still associated with some effort.

If you live in an area where the tap water is very hard, the water level indicator can easily calcify and then no longer show the actual water level. In that case, you should clean it with some vinegar.

If plants are always overfilled in hydroponic culture, they suffocate because they cannot breathe enough air. If you frequently travel for a long time, hydroponics can be problematic.

Climbing aids and supports made of wood, bamboo, and other natural materials are not suitable for hydroponics, because they begin to rot if they stand permanently in the water. For hydroponics, you should, therefore, use only plastic supports.

## Planters and pots

There is a large variety of special pots for hydroponic cultivation in the specialized trade, for which special cultivation of a permanent water-tightness of the vessels is decisive.

However, normal planters have only limited waterproof properties.

If they contain a steady level of liquid over a long period, the water often leaks.

The result is unsightly water damage at each site. The following criteria are crucial in the selection of vessels and pots:

- Ideal are separate planters for the hydroponic culture Vessels of metal and with glazes are not suitable
- Inner pot plus waterproof planter, especially for small plants

- For large plants, it is synonymous with only a large and waterproof pot
- Install the water level indicator with the associated float in the inner pot
- Professional hydroponic pots have a separate device for the water level indicator.

**JAMIE BACKYARD**

# Chapter 2:
# Types Of Hydroponic Systems

Over time, six hydroponic systems were created. They differ in how they provide a plant with three vital resources. Each hydroponic system provides the plant with water, nutrients, and oxygen. Hydroponic systems can be active or passive. The difference lies in the use of electrical components. While an active hydroponic system is powered by electric water and air pump, a passive hydroponic system is free of technical equipment.

The advantages of the active system are at the same time, the disadvantages of a passive system:

On the one hand, an air pump enriches the nutrient solution with oxygen, prevents algae growth, and promotes plant growth instead. A water pump additionally enables the commissioning of all hydroponic systems. These include very efficient and profitable operations.

On the other hand, without electrical equipment, you are independent of power sources, and you save on acquisition and electricity costs. Furthermore, a distinction is made between circulating and noncirculating systems. However, this distinction is rather secondary for hobby gardeners and is therefore only briefly explained.

In some systems, the nutrient solution repeatedly cycles through the system - it circulates. Similarly, a hydroponic system can be designed so that the nutrient solution only reaches the roots of the plant once - it does not circulate. The latter is mainly practiced commercially.

There are six different hydroponic systems. Each hydroponic system differs in how it provides water, nutrients, and oxygen to the plants. The six hydroponic systems include:

1. The Wick system
2. The deepwater culture
3. The ebb and flood system
4. The drip system
5. The nutrient film technique ( NFT )
6. The aeroponic system

Further system variations emerged from the six system types, in order to better adapt the system properties to the needs of the plants, such as the kratky method, fogponics, or the Dutch bucket system. These are explained in the detailed contributions.

## Wick system

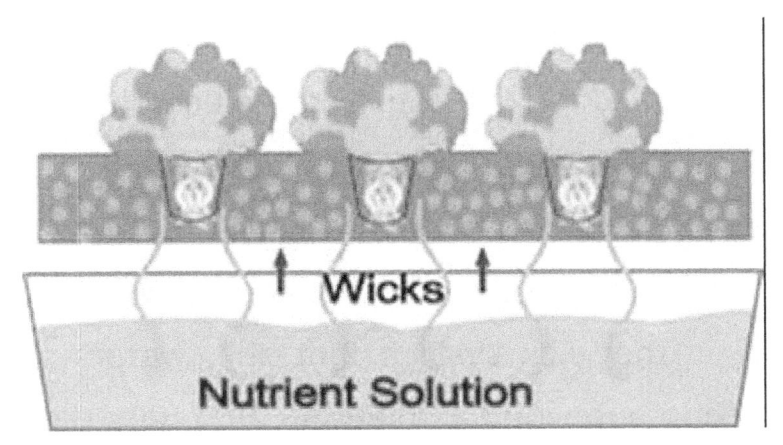

Thousands of years ago, plants were watered with a wick. The wick system sprang from traditional wick irrigation and provided the plants with a wick. The wick system is passive, easy to build, and suitable for beginners. The capillary effect (or capillary action) allows nutrient solution to rise to the roots. wick systems are easy to understand, consist of simple components, do not require extensive maintenance, and can be produced inexpensively. Although they are part of the hydroponic cultivation, they do not require any pumps or vents. The omission of these components makes wick systems the simplest form of a hydroponic plant. The whole concept of a wick system is based on the so-called capillary effect, a process in which fluids migrate against gravity using a piece of cloth or bandage. The plant provides energy to transport the solution into the roots and not the other way round. Since the plant is now the determining variable, it only takes as much water as it needs.

The wick should be long enough to immerse in the nutrient solution and allow the other end of the wick to contact the root system of your plant. In addition, the earth must be replaced by an alternative cultivation medium. Good alternatives are sand, gravel, or perlite. Each of these materials can absorb and release moisture. The choice of your medium depends on the effectiveness of your wick. The air pump is optional in the wick system, but still, waters are not only deep but also tend to oxygen depletion. Although the plants are supplied with oxygen by small pores and interstices of the substrate, they also absorb dissolved oxygen in the nutrient solution. Therefore, it is a good idea to put an air pump in the reservoir, and then the wick system is not quite so passive anymore. If the pump fails, the damage is far less severe than in other systems. Another advantage of the air pump is the constant circulation of the water, which prevents the nutrients from settling on the ground. As a wick should be best-used plastic, cotton, for example, would rot.

## Wick - system , excellent for Beginners

Why is a wick system so practical when you need expensive accessories and extensive knowledge of growing cannabis for traditional hydroponic plants? Although one should still know the basics of cannabis cultivation, wick systems will have no complications that can be a problem, especially for inexperienced growers.

With no soil in play, you do not have to worry about risks such as pests, mold, and contamination. The use of a wick provides a continuous supply of nutrient-rich water. Concerned that they might not get enough water, beginners tend to over-irrigate the plants. Wick systems passively provide the plants with only as much water as they need. Passive systems are quiet and do not require power. Although there are already complete systems on the market, a wick system can be crafted using household materials. And because it works without moving parts, the risk of breakage or other complications is incredibly low.

## The construction

Enough talk about the advantages and the concept of a hydroponic wick system. Now let's look at how you can make your own. Before we go into detail, we want to address one more important aspect; the most important factor is the quality of your wick. After all, this is the crucial factor in a wick system. The material of the wick is largely responsible for the speed and amount of liquid that it can absorb and transport to your plant.For the wick, everyday household items can be used. These include nylon cords, the fibers of a mop, strips of old clothing, or propylene — the best way to test each option before in dyed water. After at least an hour you should have an idea of how fast and far the water can be transported. For the best result, you can use two wicks per plant.

Materials that can be used as a wick:

- Lamp wick
- Felt strips
- Rayon
- Wool ropes or wool stripes
- Nylon ropes
- Cotton ropes
- The strip of a mop (new)
- Stripes of old clothes and blankets

## Manual

Fill a small bucket or container with nutrient-rich water. Ideally, the container is dark and has a slightly smaller diameter than the pot with the plant. The container serves as a reservoir, from which your plant is supplied with water and the necessary nutrients.

Then you put two wicks in the middle of the pot in which you want to grow your plant. Two small holes should be made in the bottom so that the wicks can hang down.

Fill the plant pot with the selected growing medium and make sure that the wicks are long enough to come in contact with the root system of your plants and the nutrient solution.

You may need to adjust the length of the wick. If you are satisfied, you can put the plant pot on the container of point 1. The container with the plant should now be above the water, in which a part of the wick hangs. To avoid disease or contamination, the bottom of the water reservoir should be tight. The nutrient solution should not come into contact with light or air.

Congratulations, you have just built your hydroculture wick system! Keep an eye on the nutrient solution in the reservoir to replenish it in time. How often you have to refill depends on the thirst of your plant.

## Advantages

- Easy to realize, even with plastic waste Passive without an air pump
- No pump can fail (except the optional air pump) => low maintenance, no accidents

## Disadvantage

- Not suitable for larger, thirstier plants
- The growing medium can contain nutrients, which can cause a toxic accumulation
- The water in the storage tank can become "stale"
- If the system is not cleaned regularly, mold may form
- If the water tank is closed, the oxygenation of the roots can be a problem
- The nutrient solution must be tested regularly for the correct ph value

## Deepwater culture

Deep water culture is a cultivation method in which the plants are kept floating in the nutrient solution, and the roots are suspended directly in the nutrient solution. In most cases, the plants are placed with substrate-filled mesh pots in suitably perforated styropor plates and then placed in basins with nutrient solution. Since roots need not only water and nutrients but also oxygen, the nutrient solution pool must be well ventilated so that air bubbles constantly rise. Failure to do so will cause the roots and the plants to die quickly.Deepwater cultures for growing cannabis: for beginners, the deep water culture (dwc) system is inexpensive and easy to assemble and use. A dwc setup usually consists of three parts:

- A bucket or reservoir in which the nutrient solution is stored on a water basis
- Another basket or net with peat or rockwool as "soil" so that the roots can grow through to the nutrient solution
- A submerged air stone (like a fish tank) that supplies the nutrient solution with air.

You need a dwc unit for each plant you want to grow. Imagine a 20-liter bucket of nutrient-rich water on the ground, then a hammock filled with peat or clay, in which to plant the grass, then the air stone inside the liquid bubbles upon the ground. The majority of the root system is constantly immersed in the nutrient solution.

Then imagine that you have more than one plant. In a system of many buckets, all individual buckets of irrigation hoses are connected to a single reservoir, which delivers the nutrient water for feeding the individual plants. In these larger recirculating dwc systems, there is not an air stone in each bucket that would be inefficient so that the nozzles provide oxygen to the water as it is being pumped through the system.

## Recirculating

Hydroponic systems are used very often and commercially under the hydroponic system. If one uses the technique on a larger scale, one usually uses several targets and one central source reservoir. That's how you save air stones. However, then the roots are no longer supplied directly with air bubbles, but only with oxygen dissolved in water from the central nutrient tank. Thus, increasing the amount of dissolved oxygen, the target container is flooded continuously, and by overflow water flowing to the central reservoir cascading led back. By refluxing waterfalls into the source container, additional oxygen is taken. The deeper the waterfalls, the more oxygen is supplied. Since the water in the destination container always overflows, there must be no amount of water controlled, but only in the source container. So, there is only one place where most parameters such as ph, nutrient solution concentration, water temperature, oxygen content, must be monitored and monitored. This makes the recirculating system easy to maintain.

## Why is it called deep water culture?

Two reasons: first, and most obviously, because the water in the reservoir is more in-depth than in some other hydroponic systems. In deeper waters, the nutrient content remains more stable, which makes life a little easier - less need for supervision second, because the majority of the root mass is continuously submerged in the water.

It is a very popular system in hydroponic farms. By controlling the amount and frequency of watering your plants, you will also control the nutrient intake. This allows the farmer to adapt his solution supply to the number of droplets given to a plant.

## Benefits of a deep water culture system

- Sometimes it comes to extensive root systems
- Relatively low maintenance - only one container to monitor, but regular monitoring is recommended.
- Few moving parts

- Easy to assemble
- Modular systems are easy to expand if you want to grow more.
- Good systems for beginners - most setups are turnkey solutions.

**Disadvantages of a deep water culture system**
- It can be difficult to maintain the correct water temperature in the reservoir.
- A power outage or a pump failure can be fatal to the harvest if you do not catch it quickly - without oxygen, the roots drown.
- You need a replacement pump just in case.
- A replacement can also be useful if you want to leave the water 2 or 3 days before a water change.
- Cheap pumps can be noisy - but a good pump should have indicated their noise level.
- Small dwc systems can be tricky - water evaporates more, affecting the ph. and nutrient concentration.

One last tip for dwc cultivation systems:

Two things to be careful of are pollution and stagnant water. Make sure that the nutrients on the bottom of the main tank are protected from light and dirt, and that the rock stone does not stop working.

## Drip system

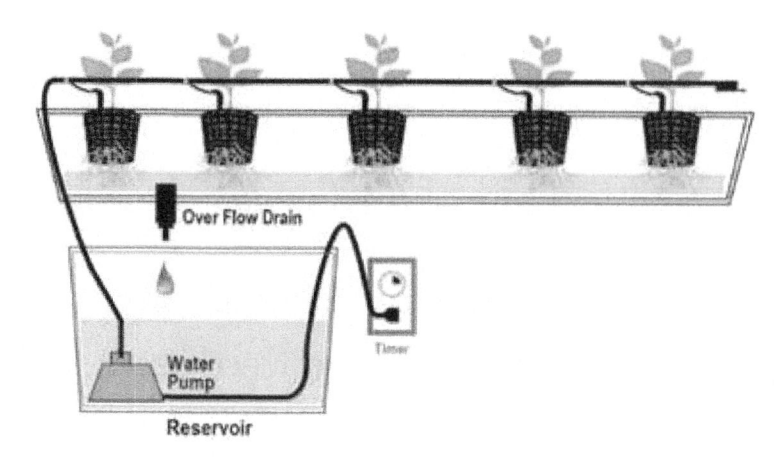

The drip irrigation system consists of a series of small pipes and droppers that connect your water tank to each of the plants in your garden. There is no limit. We could feed some plants or an industrial facility using a drip irrigation system. A timer then controls the amount of solution and the frequency of administration; neither one more drop nor one drop less is administered to the plants. You do not even have to be there to feed them. This will save you time and money, allowing you to deal with non-automated processes. In more conventional plantations, water is usually given in excess to the plant. It is expected to flow. This is not the best way for a plant to grow, nor the most environmentally friendly. This system still has its disadvantages. This will not be the easiest method to set up. Having a garden hose around your grow room will make things much easier for the average grower. Hoses should also be cleaned from time to time to prevent clogging. Algae and mineral buildup could stop the flow of water.

This could result in one or more of your plants not getting the water solution they need. If your system distributes water under the soil, you will have no way of knowing if your plant is being nourished. You will notice a nutrient deficiency only a few days later.

Drip irrigation will also require monthly rinsing. This will help solve this problem. By regularly rinsing your system, you will clean the residue left by the slow flow of water. The frequency of this operation will depend on the cleanliness of your kit, the quality of your water, and your nutrient solution. Finally, although this system requires less supervision, it requires more attention when you face it. You will need to constantly check your plants for signs of poor health or disease. This is the only way to solve a problem in time. Particularly important for farmers living in extremely dry areas where water may be scarce. Drip irrigation will ensure you always have enough water for your plants.


## The materials you need to manufacture your own drop-inlet irrigation system

To make your own drip irrigation system, you will need a transmitter for each plant. This is what controls the water supply of each plant. There are many variations in these products. Some are simply a perforated pipe allowing the evacuation of water. Others come attached to a plastic pile and spread the water over a larger area. It's up to you to decide which method is the best. What you must look for are transmitters with pressure compensation. This is because if you have multiple levels in your grow room, those in the lower level will end up receiving more water due to gravity. Pressure compensation guarantees the same power on every installation, regardless of elevation variations.

You will need pipes to enter the transmitters. This will ensure that the water reaches your plant. These will then be connected to a pvc collector that will serve as a platform for your water supply. The size will vary according to the number of plants. In a large-scale operation, you will need not only a longer but thicker pvc pipe. With all this, your next purchase will be a water pump. Most pumps on the market do a good job, pumping over 1,000 liters of water per hour, which is more than enough.

The last most neglected material is the bucket. This is very important because it is where the excess water flows. Your pump will then reuse this water, saving you money, and paying attention to the environment.

Now let's put all these materials together and assemble them in a functional drip irrigation system.

## Build your drop irrigation system - prepare materials

The great trick about drip irrigation is that it requires almost no extra money or effort to add another plant to your garden. Today we will install a straightforward installation. Since it is super easy and quick to build, this technique will not accommodate an industrial plant for professional farmers. It's perfect for people like you and me who want a few plants so we can grow our own grass and share it with our friends and family.

You will first need some kind of bucket or container, listed as the last material above. Look for one with a lid. The size of the bucket determines the number of plants you can accommodate in your system. You will need to adjust the net, so cut appropriately sized holes in the lid of your bucket. These will have a diameter of about 10-12 cm. Drill another hole large enough to pass the pump outlet. The last hole to be made should be the diameter of the thick pipe connected to the pump.

Now that everything is ready, let's start building.

Place the pump at the bottom of the bucket and run the hose through the lid. The next step will be to reduce the 1.2 cm hose so that the pump is compatible with a size that will not flood your plants. You will need a reducer that decreases the pipe in half. This will certainly meet your needs better. Then place the lid on the bucket.

Push the hose inside the hole so that the gearbox remains flat on top. Blow, the hardest is gone. Once the reducer is at the end of the thicker pipe, attach 10 cm of one of the thinnest pipes to the other end.

Now all you have to do is place your pots in the holes provided for this purpose and fill them with your growing media, such as clay balls or rockwool. Finally, you can place your seed or clone. Make sure the pipe is there, and you are ready. Plug in and wait for the results to appear. Remember to include a timer on your outlet so that it does not work 24 hours a day. The ideal scenario will be about 3 times a day for 6 minutes. Remember to check that there are no clogged transmitters, and you will not be disappointed with the final product. This is a system requiring very little maintenance and has the potential to give you higher quality returns. Have fun, and do not forget to learn from your mistakes.

## Hydroponics with drops (top feed)

In a hydroponic drip irrigation system, the nutrient solution is slowly released directly to the roots via a network of tubes inserted into the growth medium. The solution continually drips or is sprayed into the medium and slowly drains through the root system so that it can be returned to the reservoir. However, the drain can also be routed directly into the waste, which is more expensive and less environmentally friendly, but provides optimal nutrition and protects against fungal infections. The upper system is often used for tillage and can be part of a dwc system.

## Advantages of a top-feed/drip grow system

Very efficient use of water and nutrients, saving on operating costs

Suitable for areas with water scarcity

Good, if you have to pay attention to the budget

No or less regular emptying and replacement of the container necessary

Few moving parts

Low maintenance, which has a large reservoir that can be run over a more extended period of time.

Disadvantages of a top-feed/drip grow system

Emitters tend to clog up - and you'll usually notice it when a plant starts to wilt or has other signs of malnutrition.

Not good for organic farming

Pumps that are used for recirculation can break, so you need to have a spare part handy again.

The timer for controlling the drop flow can also go awry.

## Ebb and flood

Ebb and flood systems periodically soak and drain the roots of the plants. You do not have to worry about using air stones because the water does not stagnate. And also, the root system gets plenty of air because the solution evaporates. You need a timer if the system is not included. Again, if your central reservoir has a parasitic or imbalance problem, all plants will suffer.

## Different designs

Plant containers in series. The containers are located above the reservoir so that gravity can be used after the flood to ebb. First, the containers are connected to pipes so that all containers are filled evenly and simultaneously when flooding. There simply is not an inlet and an overflow for each container, just a central inlet, and an overflow. The height of the overflow determines the maximum height of the water level in all containers.

Box design. This system is used for the temporary stay of plants, e.g., during cultivation. There is only one box, again above the reservoir, to use gravity for the return flow. In this box are smaller pots with plants and substrate, which are surrounded by water at high tide. This box contains only one inflow and one outflow. The disadvantage of this design is that light can fall unhindered into the flooding water, and so algae can grow well. Algae extract water from the water, which is already scarce at high tide. Trough tank design. This system is used when there is little vertical space available, and the reservoir is under crop buckets. Containers have the same water level when connected to a common pipe below the water surface. This effect uses the trough tank design. The water level in the buckets is determined by the flood tank, which is connected to the buckets. In the flood condition, water is pumped from the reservoir into the flood tank. If the water level in the tide tank rises above a certain level, water is pumped back from the trough simultaneously (flood condition, both pumps running). If the water is to be shed again, only the pump is running, which pumps the water back into the reservoir.

## Advantages of ebb and flood/flood and drainage systems
- Pretty easy to use
- Flooding periods help prevent root rot
- Highly productive

## Disadvantages of low tide and high tide and drainage of growing systems
- The water must be changed every few days in the circulatory system (so it might be worth investing in a replacement reservoir).
- Does not grow vertically, as the crop buckets must be at the same height
- Higher operating costs through frequent water and nutrient exchange - especially in a "run to waste" system
- Replacement pump and timer required in case of error
- Relatively high maintenance

## Aeroponics with fog

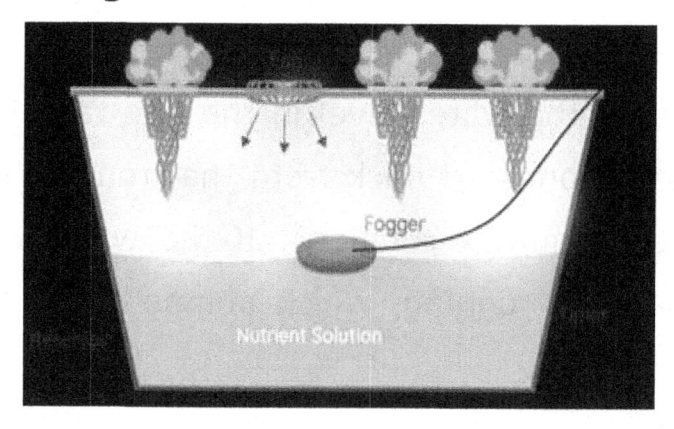

With aeroponics and misting, you have a rainforest-like atmosphere for the roots of your plants. The plants hang in baskets, and their roots are often fogged, creating a mist of nutrients. This ensures fast growth and high yields, but you have to watch everything closely. In a true aeroponic system, the root mist chamber is kept separate from the reservoir, but there are hybrid systems where the two chambers are combined.

## Why prefer aeroponics to hydroponics?

The main attraction of an aeroponic system is that it can be even more effective than a hydroponic system. The main advantage is the oxygenation of the roots, which greatly improves their growth. Besides, as a fine mist is used, nutrients are absorbed much more efficiently, which results in lesser fertilizer intake. It is much easier to set up an aeroponic system than a hydroponic system.

You can find virtually everything you need at your local DIY store to install an aeroponic system, while a hydroponic system often requires highly specialized equipment. There is also the fact that cannabis plants in an aeroponic system are much easier to transplant. As there is no culture substrate, the plants do not undergo shock during transplantation in another aeroponic system. This can be a huge advantage for growers with large amounts of growing seedlings - enough to give them much more flexibility. An aeroponic culture can be observed in its entirety without disturbing the plants. This makes it much easier to determine nutrient solution mixtures as well as to identify and resolve any potential problems before they are out of control. Although the aeroponic systems offer many advantages, they also have disadvantages. For example, ph control must be much more precise in an aeroponic system because the roots are much more vulnerable. This is why aeroponic systems should only be considered by experienced and confident growers, even if these systems are, in theory, much better.

**Aeroponics is not for beginners**

But if it's just hydroponic crops that are new to you - you already have experience with conventional cannabis cultivation - and you're not afraid of technical maintenance such as replacing pumps, hoses, and canisters. Aeroponics grow system is worth it to get the hang of it. Aeroponics is one of the most efficient and productive ways.

## There are three types of aeroponic systems

Low-pressure systems: these systems are not the real and genuine aeroponic systems because they work with little pressure. In this variant, the system is not much more complicated than the other hydroponic systems. Because it can be used as a normal aquarium pump. In addition, one uses ordinary spray heads, as they are used in other irrigation systems. It should be noted, however, that with each spray head, the pressure to be supplied increases, and the pump must be dimensioned accordingly. It is best to position the spray heads above the roots, and then the water will roll off at the roots, thus providing care to the root tips, while roots may cover the roots under the roots. Low-pressure systems are the most popular among aeroponic systems because of the smaller technical challenge, especially with hobby hydroponics. From the spray heads, no ultrafine mist comes, as in the right aeroponic system, but rather fine water jets. Thus, the size of the water drops is very different from the high-pressure systems. The roots and the substrate get wet, and so are irrigation cycles of 15 min (15 min pump on, 15 min pump off) or 30 min usual. Because it takes until the water in the root area dried again. 15 min pump off) or 30 min usual. Because it takes until the water in the root area dried again. 15 min pump off) or 30 min usual. Because it takes until the water in the root area dried again. High-pressure systems: these systems are the true aeroponic systems and operate at 4 to 6 bar, i.e., the pressure of a well-inflated bicycle tire. Since a very fine mist with very small drops of water is produced in the high-pressure system, more frequent spraying cycles, at the latest 5 minutes, are necessary. Thus, a short life of a pump is avoided by constant switching on and off, and the pump is eliminated from the system. Instead, one uses an accumulator tank similar to that used in the reverse osmosis water system and valves. The pressure is always maintained in the tank, while the fog is generated in the root area every 5 min for a few seconds.

Ultrasonic nebulizers: ultrasonic nebulizers are used in medicine for the inhalation of medications; they are also used for effective room design, humidification, and in steam baths. Ultrasonic nebulizers are also used for keeping reptiles to achieve optimum humidity. In the aeroponic system, however, they achieve mixed results. While they produce very fine water droplets, there is very little real moisture in the mist. In addition, the fog tends to fall in drops to the ground rather than wet the roots for a few minutes.

## Advantages of an aeroponic cultivation system

Lowest and most efficient use of water compared to other systems - aeroponics is a circulatory system with very low water evaporation.

Fastest growing system

Some of the highest hydroponic yields (10x more than ground) - aeroponics creates ideal root growth

Roots in constant contact with oxygen

Very low probability of algae, as no light, penetrates the root zone.

Relatively disease-free environment

Plants can grow closer together for more efficient use of space, as root networks do not compete for space.

## Disadvantages of an aeroponic cultivation system

- You must already be familiar with growing cannabis so you can identify and fix problems early.
- Very low margins of error! Plants grow faster, but also wither faster if something goes wrong.
- Much attention to detail required
- Ideally, you should have monitoring systems that alert you to problems so that you can respond within an hour (so long it takes for the roots to dry out and the plants begin to die).
- Electricity runs 24/7
- Pumps and timers may fail.
- More technical, more moving parts than other systems
- Not great for growing in a closet or spare bedroom, unless you have an extremely well-insulated grow tent.

## Nutrient film technique

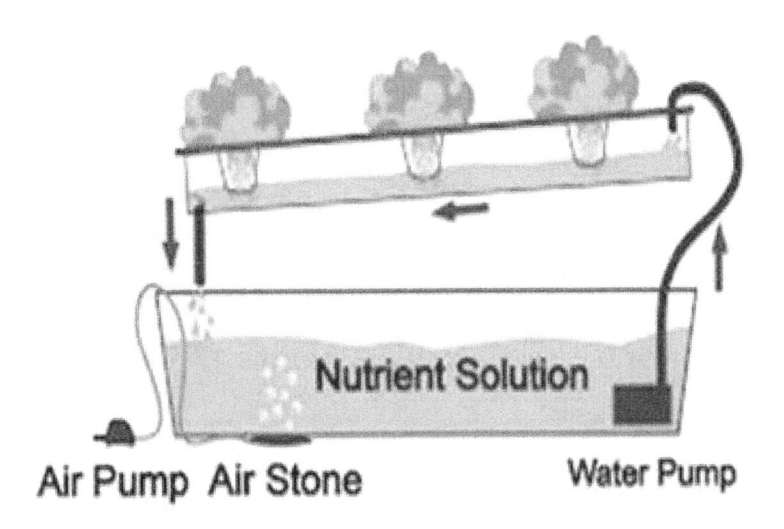

In nutrient film technology, some roots of the plant are in the nutrient solution, while large parts are only in the air. The plant is thus ideally supplied with the optimal mixture of nutrients and oxygen. As soon as young plants have formed sufficiently long roots, they are put into the plant tube (gully, canal) together with the netting and substrate. In this circulatory system, the nutrient solution is pumped from the reservoir into the canal. The nutrient solution then flows in a thin film down the slightly angled channel into the return flow that flows back to the source container.

The nft system is perceived as pleasantly easy and often used commercially. However, there are some principles to be followed for the growth of the plants to succeed.

## Shape

The usual height for the canal is 4 - 5 cm. The roots do not grow in-depth but in width. The width is determined depending on the expected root mass.

10 cm for a short time growing plants such as lettuce or herbs 15 cm for a long time growing and small plants like strawberries

20 cm or more for a long time growing plants that form large roots, such as the tomato

The channel is professionally not round, as many hobby gardeners do, but square. In a round tube, the nutrient solution is unevenly distributed, so that only a few roots are supplied with a nutrient solution. In a square channel, the entire soil is covered with a nutrient solution, and more roots can absorb nutrients and water.

## Gradient

A gradient of 1:16 is recommended. This means that for a 16 at the long gully, the height difference is 1 cm. Theoretically, the gradient could be 1: 100 cm. In practice, however, then congestion forms, which contradict the principle of the system, only to produce a film of nutrient solution.

## Throughput

For 10 cm wide channels, a throughput of 0.5 l per minute is recommended for wide channels 2 l.

The gradient also affects the thickness of the film. The film should be neither too deep nor too shallow.

## Length

The length of the channel from the inlet of the nutrient solution to its outflow is limited. If the canal is too long, the supply of nutrients and oxygen for all plants can no longer be maintained. The length of the gully depends on the gradient and throughput. As a rule of thumb, it should not be more than 10 to 15 meters, or it should be pumped after this length at the latest fresh nutrient solution.

## Advantages

Particularly good ratio of nutrients, oxygen, and water

The operation of the system is simple once it is set up and has the right design

No timer or pump control needed, the pump just runs through

No medium required, as the plant only needs to be held at one point and hang in the roots in air and water.

## Disadvantage

If the pump fails and there is no replacement pump, the harvest is quickly gone, as there is only the thin film nutrient solution

Not necessarily suitable for plants with big roots

The system is prone to blockage by abundant root growth and congestion. But with the right design (shape, slope, throughput, length), this can be prevented.

# Chapter 3:
# Hydroponics Growing Medium

The most important hydroponics growing medium are the following:
- Perlite
- Clay ball or expanded clay ball
- Vermiculite
- Rockwool
- Rice husks
- Pumice
- Jute substrate
- Coconut
- Sand
- Gravel
- Wood chips
- Hemp substrate
- Neoprene plug substrate
- Expanded clay spheres substrate
- Eazy plug substrate
- Peat substrates

## Perlite

Appearing as tiny round white dots in the midst of the other components, perlite in the soil is a non-organic additive used to aerate media. Vermiculite is also an additive to the soil used for aeration (although less so than perlite), but the two are not always interchangeable, although they provide the same benefit as means of rooting.

Other uses of perlite include masonry construction, cement and gypsum plasters, and loose insulation. Perlite is also used in pharmaceutical products and in the filtration of water in communal pools, as well as in abrasives for polishes, detergents, and soaps.

Perlite is a form of volcanic glass ($SiO_2$) that is extracted all over the world. Perlite is an amorphous volcanic glass that has a relatively high water content, typically formed by the hydration of obsidian. It occurs naturally and has the unusual property of expanding considerably when heated sufficiently. It is an industrial mineral and a commercial product useful for its low density after processing.

Perlite is extracted using open-hole methods such as tearing or blasting, or both. If perlite is soft and brittle, brecciated, or widely articulated, the tear is used with significant cost savings. Blasting is necessary where perlite cannot be easily broken using rippers, but care must be taken to achieve fragmentation without producing excessive fines or oversized material.

## Horticultural perlite

Although both perlite and vermiculite promote water retention, perlite is the most porous and tends to allow water to drain much more quickly than vermiculite. As such, it is a more suitable addition to soils used with plants that do not require very wet soils, such as cactus soils, or plants that generally thrive in well-draining soils.

Horticultural perlite is produced by exposing perlite to heat, which causes the trace water contained in perlite to expand, "popping" the perlite as popcorn and expanding it to 13 times its previous size, resulting in an incredibly light material. In fact, the final product weighs only 5 to 8 pounds per cubic foot. Overheated perlite is composed of tiny air compartments. Under a microscope, perlite is revealed to be covered by many tiny cells that absorb moisture outside the particle, not inside, which makes it particularly useful for facilitating moisture to plant roots. The result is a very light white stone-like substance. Perlite is appreciated for its moisture retention and aeration properties. It is naturally sterile and has a neutral ph.

## Use of perlite for plants

In principle, it is used in the same way and at the same place where vermiculite and sand are used, often combined with these materials. In addition to adding perlite to the soil for plants, it can still be used as:

Mulch. It will not only retain moisture but also prevent the formation of a solid crust on the surface of the earth. Perlite cake not like sand.

Medium for seed germination. In this respect, it is much better than all other materials and blends. Perlite is suitable for air and moisture. It can, therefore, be used for germinating seeds, which are not recommended to be sprinkled after sowing. This does not apply to perlite.

The pearls are very useful for rooting cuttings of plants that require moderate humidity, but not allowed (azalea, hydrangea, etc.).

Drainage. Agro-perlite can be used as a separate drainage layer and as an extra layer of expanded clay, for example.

Humidifier. Drawn wet perlite provides the necessary moisture balance on the plant.

Pure, dry perlite is an excellent material for storing wintering tubers and flower bulbs (gladioli, for example). And not just flowers. In this material, it is good to store vegetables (mainly root vegetables). This is only the most important list of uses of perlite for home plants. If you want, you can continue.

## Characteristics of perlite application

Although the composition of pearlite contains various microelements that are necessary for plants, they are all in a bound state and do not reach the plants. That is why the use of perlite does not exclude the fertilization of plants.

Although perlite is neutral, if you use hard water to irrigate plants, it will shift from the neutral to the alkaline side. For some plants, this is not very good. With the use of rain, snow, or softened water, no alkalization of perlite occurs.

## Most important benefits

It is completely clean and sterile from a biological point of view, without the microorganism content. It is very light and is often used instead of sand for plants with a weakened root system. Perlite retains moisture well and evenly releases it to the roots. Because this material, unlike sand, does not settle, it offers excellent moisture and air permeability.

The surface of the earth with perlite is never covered with a hard crust. Due to the thermal insulation properties of perlite, the root system of plants does not cool or does not overheat.

## Clay ball

The expanded clay ball is used as an inert substrate, pure or mixed, for hydroponic cultivation. But it is interesting to know where it comes from to understand its functions and benefits in hydroponics. The clay ball is first in the form of clay, natural rocky material, and then shaped into balls. Placed in a high-temperature oven, heated to 1200°C, the clay balls expand and form very porous beads. All clay balls are not identical, and their density can vary from 0.5 to more than 1 g/cm3. There are also different sizes: 4-8 and 8-16.

### What are the benefits of the clay ball?
- Stable substrate
- Easy and fast use
- Optimum drainage quality
- 100% natural substrate
- Usable in decoration

## The clay ball as a substrate in hydroponics

The big advantage of the clay ball is that it does not retain water; it is ideal in hydroponics. Indeed, it has a closed internal porosity, that is, the air or the nutrient solution cannot penetrate the beads. Irrigation can be continuous without drowning crops.

## Vermiculite

The growth medium vermiculite is a silicate mineral that just as perlite expands when exposed to very high temperatures. The mineral is inflated under high heat (like popcorn). This results in a brittle material which, among other things, is used for insulation. If growth media vermiculite perlite resembles except that it has a relatively high cation exchange capacity, that means they are light, they insulate well and take a lot of moisture to slowly then off. There are different types of applications and vermiculite. It is so important that you should make sure that you use vermiculite intended for horticulture. The easiest way to make sure it is to buy it from a nursery.

Vermiculite is a mineral that, when heated rapidly, exceeds 900 degrees exfoliates as a harmonica and becomes several times larger than the original ore. A very light, non-flammable, inert, highly heat-resistant insulation material is created.

The material acquires a multi-layered lattice-like structure, such as pages of a book, separated by layers of air. In this way, a huge surface magnification has been created that is highly absorbent. It is also completely asbestos-free.

Vermiculite is a pure natural product; it has no negative environmental impact and is non-flammable. We supply vermiculite with the rhp quality mark. This quality mark is necessary in the substrate market and guarantees

that the substrate meets the exact quality requirements for the water and air content and, for example, ph values. Rhp-certified substrates ensure an optimal start of the cultivation. The raw material (vermiculite) that can be processed in potting soil (depending on the recipe of the potting soil) is available from us.

## Different grain sizes

- Superfine: 0 - 1 mm
- Fine: 1 - 2 mm
- Medium: 2 - 4 mm Large  > 8 mm

One hundred liters of vermiculite weighs
approx. 7 - 9 kg, depending on the grain size.

## Characteristics

- Mineral inorganic raw material
- No negative environmental impact

- Odorless
- Flammable
- Chemically inert, rot-free, does not mold
- High resilience and moisture absorption through open cell structure
- Asbestos-free
- Seeds germinate better
- Rapid rooting
- Carrier for water and nutrients

## Composition and properties

Suitable for taking in large amounts of water. It also easily releases moisture to the roots of plants when the substrate dries. 10 g of vermiculite retains up to 50 ml of liquid. It maintains the necessary moisture in the soil for proper rooting and growth of the seedling.

Keeps ions of nutrients that give in water into the soil with water-soluble fertilizers. These microelements accumulate and are gradually absorbed by the root system. Thus, the roots are not burned, and there is no risk of plant accumulation of radionuclides and nitrates.

Improves the mechanical composition of the soil, makes it lose, permeable to air. The scaly structure of the mineral retains air in large quantities.

The soil with agro-vermiculite is not caked and is not covered with a hard crust. Therefore, there is no need for frequent release.

Limits the appearance of pests. It is used in the fight against snails and snails. The flaky structure with dust particles repels these pests from plants.

Mineral with environmentally friendly composition contains no heavy metals.

It contains a large number of minerals: aluminum, potassium, sodium, calcium, iron, silicon. The disadvantage is that they are in a plant that is difficult to digest. That is why agro-vermiculite is not a fertilizer.

The abnormal introduction of a mineral into the soil changes the acidity in an alkaline environment. This also happens when watering the beds with hard tap water.

When applied to the ground, it improves its structure. Treats the composition as follows:

Absorbs salts of heavy metals, radionuclides, and gas exchange products, thereby cleansing the soil. At a salt concentration of more than 12 g/m$^3$, the plant experiences intense stress, and growth is inhibited; at a concentration of 20 g/m$^3$ - the culture dies.

Improves the structure of clay soils, makes it light, crumbly, and airy. Without it, in such areas, clay particles tightly adjoin each other after the rain.

The soil becomes air and moisture resistant, with drought, it forms a hard crust on the soil. The rate of agro-vermiculite administration is 2 liters per 1 m3 of soil.

Deoxidizes the soil. Soil with an acidic reaction is unsuitable for growing most vegetable, fruit, and ornamental crops. Use the mineral to neutralize the ph to 5.5-6.5 in a 1: 1 mixture with perlite. Use 0.5 buckets of mixture per 1 m² of the ground surface.

Extensive agro-vermiculite is widely used in gardening and vegetable growing.

1. For growing seeds. In the open soil, vermiculite is applied to a bed or well at a rate of 250 ml per 50 cm² of the soil surface. It is also possible to germinate seeds from flowers and vegetables for seedlings in pure vermiculite. The seeds germinate faster than in the soil of peat and chernozem. Thanks to the porous structure of the mineral, the seeds are protected against the "blackleg" and other diseases.

2. Additive to the soil mixture. Optimal volume - up to 30% of the total weight of the landing mix. It is recommended to use it with torch, peat, and sand. In this ratio, optimum soil moisture is maintained even in the event of drought.

3. For mulching the ground. Agro-vermiculite protects the top layer of the soil against rapid drying. There is no crust on it, which prevents moisture and air.

For mulching adult plants, large and medium-sized vermiculite is used at a dosage of 5 liters per 1 m2 of land for flower crops - up to 2 liters per 1 m². Council. Vermiculite, as a mulch, is embedded in the top layer of the soil. Otherwise, it flies around the site in windy weather.

4. As a heat-insulating material. Addition to the ground and mulching with agro-vermiculite protects young seedlings and seedlings from spring, ground frost. It also protects plants against overheating in the summer and helps overwinter during severe frosts. The consumption rate, when added to the plant pit, is a maximum of 30% of the source volume. When mulching the soil, add a layer of vermiculite in 1-2 cm.

5. To store the harvest of fruit and vegetables. Agro-vermiculite is unable to absorb moisture from the air. That is why it maintains the necessary humidity in the box and prevents decay. It also preserves the taste of fruit and vegetables, slows the growth of roots in bulbs. Sprinkle each layer of fruit, vegetables, or bulbs in

a box with a vermiculite layer of 5 cm.

6. For compost. Compost is made from litter, bird droppings, peat, grass, and stems from some garden crops. The use of 10 liters of vermiculite per 30 kg of organic improves the structure of the resulting composition.

## Rockwool

The rockwool hydroponic growing medium is one of the most common growth media used in hydroponics. Rock wool is a sterile, porous, non- degradable agent which consists mainly of granite and/or limestone, which is first heated by heat and then melts and then spun into small wires as cotton candy. The mineral wool is then formed into blocks, sheets, cubes, plates, or other shapes. Rockwool suck water easily, so you must be careful that it is not too wet, so you suffocate plant roots or get rot and root rot. You must also bring the wool at the proper ph before you use it. This is done by soaking can make water acidic to neutral ph water. Je it by adding lemon juice. A lemon is naturally changing the ph. Most plants like ph 5.5-6. Test after adding plant food. Give water only when the pot feels light. You wet the plug before hoards. Do not forget to add a small number of nutrients in the water.

Rock wool substrate produced from minerals at high temperatures, very light, with high porosity.

Very cheap and, therefore, widely used. Disadvantages are fiber dusts during handling, uneven moisture in the substrate, no optimal oxygen supply.

Not compostable

Rockwool is made from basalt, a solid rock, that is spun into an air-filled absorbent fiber, similar to fiberglass or wool. Although it can be supplied in the form of small cubes, it is usually packaged in long, narrow plastic sleeves to form a rod 6 inches wide, 3 inches deep and 40 inches long, called a slice. Plates can be reused for up to three seasons if they are properly sterilized.

**Things you need**
- Utility knife
- Work gloves
- Face mask
- Wallpaper steamer
- Plastic covers
- Tarp

**Steps to use a rock wool medium**

Cut the plastic sleeve from the rock wool with a knife.

Place the tiles on end and lean them against a wall or fence to dry.

Put on gloves and a disposable mask. Dry rock wool is irritating to the skin, just like fiberglass, and can create dust in the air.

Remove or scrape as much as possible dead, dried root material from the previous crop.

Examine the plates. Do not use broken or crumbling objects that have lost more than 10 percent of their depth.

Stack the plates on an old pallet or other structure that causes them to get off the ground to allow air circulation. Layer the plates in a log cabin formation with two plates perpendicular to each other, then the next two on top of the first in the opposite direction so that the ends intersect. Repeat for as many slices as you need to sterilize.

Cover the stack with a canvas and put it under the pallet on three sides, making sure that the fourth side falls on the floor.

Fill a wallpaper steamer according to the manufacturer's instructions.

Insert the hose end of the steamer under the tarpaulin so that its mouth lies in the center of the stack of plates. Insert the fourth side of the sail near the hose.

Let the steamer run for at least 30 minutes to ensure that all fungi, bacteria, or nematodes that have collected the plates are killed.

Switch off the steamer and allow the heat to evaporate before removing the tarpaulin and allowing the plates to cool and dry.

Pack the dry plates in new plastic sleeves for reuse.

## Rice husks

An organic and sustainable substrate is rice husk. These cover the rice and are a waste product of the rice industry.

In recent years, growers are increasingly looking for viable ways to reduce production costs and sustainability. The question is whether this parboiled rice hulls, a popular option is for greenhouse cultivation as a growth medium.

In principle, there is a good reason. This "cooked rice" can environmental growers, horticultural, and economic advantages when processed according to strict specifications without reducing the quality of the plant. Therefore, they are available as pure rice husks packaged in compressed bales or premixed and ready to use at major manufacturers without soil mix. These so-called pbh are consistent in size and shape.

Only the rice hulls of parboiled rice should be used because they are sterile and free of pests. Parboiling is an industrial process in which the rice is precooked. This kills all harmful bacteria and organisms.

The ph of parboiled rice is between 5.5 and 6.5. This range is perfect for most plants in hydroponics. The rice hulls can be easily composted after use.

An essential advantage of parboiled rice hulls is that it has been sterilized and free of viable weed seeds. Perlite and pbh produce results comparable to plant growth and root systems. Rice husks increase the air pore space and porosity in the growth medium. They also have a slightly higher capacity to retain water than perlite.

It is the perfect substitute for perlite. In the tree nursery, parboiled rice hulls is used as a container-top dress to prevent weed seeds from the air to achieve the mix. Parboiled rice hulls nature's media amendment lowers freight costs, generates less waste, and minimizes the storage and processing. It is a natural byproduct of rice and a renewable resource with much to offer gardeners, nurserymen, consumers, and the environment.

Unlike perlite, pumice, vermiculite, and others, rice husks are good for adding organic material, but you must reapply annually to get the other benefits of moisture management and ventilation.

## Advantages

- Good drainage
- Decomposes relatively slowly
- Compostable
- Lower cost base than perlite

- Creates optimum porosity, stability, drainage
- Requires little or no modification of fertility and irrigation
- Dramatically less dusty than perlite
- About a third less than needed supplies perlite-7 parboiled rice hulls -trucks versus 10 perlite
- Less cargo, labor, storage and packaging
- Natural color blends well with other media components

## Disadvantage

- Relatively high manganese content. (unproblematic as long as the ph is above 5.5)
- Cannot be reused
- Must be renewed regularly
- Ph value of 5.5 - 6.5

## Pumice

The word pumice is derived from the Latin word pumex, which means "foam" pumice stone is a pyroclastic material (meaning that it is formed from the volcanic matter), solidified rock. The chemical properties of pumice vary between deposits, but it is mainly composed of amorphous aluminum silicate (silica), aluminum oxide, and trace amounts of other oxides such as iron and iron oxide, sodium oxide, calcium oxide, and magnesium oxide. Its pale, light color, ranging from white to gray to greenish-brown, indicates that this volcanic rock has a high silicon dioxide content and contains little iron and magnesium. Pumice has a vesicular matrix structure with mainly two types of vesicles. These are namely tubular microvesicles and spherical or subferic vesicles. With a porosity of 90%, pumice is also the only known stone that floats on water. However, after absorbing sufficient amounts of water, it will eventually even sink.

## Jute substrate

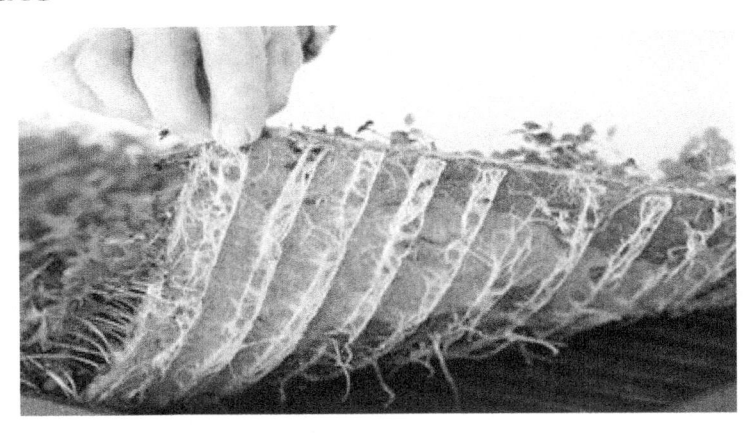

Jute fibers mainly consist of the plant substances cellulose and lignin and fall into the category of best fibers. Like natural fibers, jute fibers are entirely biodegradable. Jute has a high resistance to algae and fungi, is ph-neutral. Jute plugs as a substrate have a high water retention capacity and a very open structure for good root oxygenation. Plus, it is compostable and has no contamination of the nutrient solution.

## Coconut

Coconut chips or coconut granules are from the coconut bark. The difference between the coconut fibers is the size of the particles. Different is, therefore, the air-water ratio. The coconut substrate is obtained as a byproduct in the processing of coconut shells. Short fibers are dried and pressed into shaped bodies. As a result, it can be transported very compact. The addition of water produces about 14 liters of coconut substrate from 1 kg of the pressed material. A disadvantage is often high and strongly fluctuating salinity, which must be considered in hydroponic cultivation. As a substrate, it has been proven in many applications. Compostable. Because coconut chips or coconut granules are relatively coarse-grained, the roots are very well supplied with oxygen. This, in turn, results in poor water retention. However, the moderate cation exchange capacity deserves special mention. Accordingly, nutrients can be well absorbed and rereleased when needed. This is also helpful for germination. In the size of the particles, however, not recommended.

## Advantages

- Stores nutrients
- Good air supply

## Disadvantage

- Swims very easily
- Dries up quickly
- Ph value of 5.5 - 6.5

## Sand

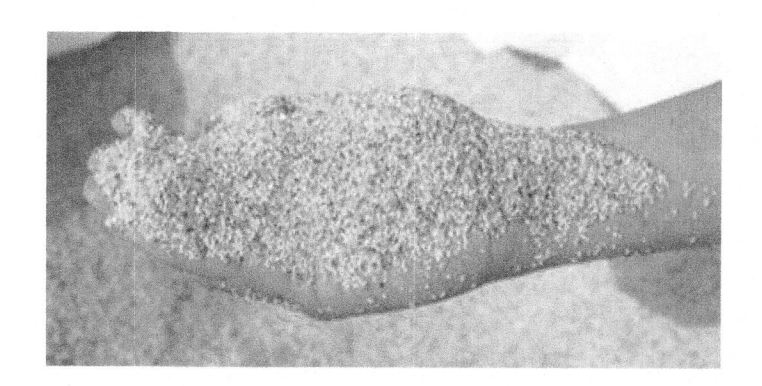

It is probably the oldest substrate of hydroponics. In addition to gravel, sand was the first substrate of hydroponics. There are now better substrates. Nowadays, sand is mostly used as a substrate only for larger plants or trees. Sand is very cheap or available for free. For those who need a substrate quickly and easily and is just right for them. Sand come from the grinding of rocks (granite, basalt, hard limestone) or are extracted from river sediments. Coarse sand may be used after the removal of fine sand and gravel. On the other hand, its capacity for retention in water is weak. Finally, they are high- density materials, and their exchange capacity is zero. It promotes drainage and prevents mixtures from clumping together. Both horticultural sand and construction sand can be used, but limestone sand should be avoided. The sand is weighty and is most often replaced by perlite and vermiculite. However, it is possible to fill the bottom of the containers if there is a threat of tipping. Sand can be used as a minor ingredient in tank, drip, wick, and tide table systems. The fineness of its grain, together with its high weight, makes it tend to migrate to the bottom of the container over time.

However, sand badly stores air and relatively little water. Sand can be mixed with perlite or expanded clay to increase air storage capacity. Likewise, when purchasing a large grain size should be taken to increase the air pockets.

In addition to the high weight, the application is also disadvantageous. Before use, the sand must be thoroughly rinsed and sterilized to remove any dust particles and organic matter. For beginners, therefore, "lighter" substrates such as rockwool or coconut fibers are better suited because these defects tolerate better in cultivation and are easier to handle. Then, sand is suitable for drip systems and ebb and flood systems.

## Advantages
- Cheap

## Disadvantage
- Heavy
- Cumbersome to handle
- Ph value depends on the mineral content

## Gravel

Gravel is coarse-grained sand. Originally gravel was widely used in ebb and flood systems due to its good drainage - until today. Due to its relatively large particles, a lot of air or oxygen gets into the interstices. While this is good for air intake, it causes water to be stored poorly and expire quickly. With gravel, there is the danger that the roots get too little water and dehydrate quickly. However, this can be beneficial for plants from dry climates. Gravel can be sterilized and therefore reused. Besides, it is cheap or free. When building the system, the high weight of the pebbles must be taken into account.

## Advantages

- Cheap or free
- Good for ebb and flood systems
- Good to try

## Disadvantage

- Heavy
- Dries up quickly
- Ph value depends on the mineral content

## Wood chips

Wood shavings can also be used as a substrate of hydroponics. Attention, do not mistake wood shavings with sawdust. Sawdust is much finer and would become too firm with water.

The coarser the wood shavings, the better the ventilation of the roots. Chips can store water relatively well. However, these should not be permanently in the water, because they would otherwise rot. Therefore, always pay attention to good drainage (for example, the ebb and flood system). The best way to buy wood chips is at the pet store or in the feeders. Buy only 100% organic chips, without any other chemical additives.

## Advantages
- Organic
- Cheap or free

## Disadvantage

- Can cause pests
- Rots with time
- Ph value is neutral

## Hemp substrate

Hemp fibers belong to the renewable raw materials, which are also grown in Germany, and are very robust natural fibers. They are completely biodegradable. As a substrate, hemp fibers are mainly used in the form of mats. They have a high pore volume and water retention capacity and are odourless. No contamination by the fiber. Compostable.

## Neoprene plug substrate

Organic, but synthetically produced are the neoprene plugs. They serve to fix the plant in the netting pot. They have no water storage capacity, but are well suited for aeroponic planting systems, as the roots are completely free. But they are also used in nft/dwc planting systems. They are reusable but not compostable.

## Expanded clay spheres substrate

Spheroidal clay is fired at high temperatures. It creates stable, porous balls that can partially float. The water storage is low, but the air content of the bed and the drainability are very high. Use should be made of ph-neutral varieties. They are easy to use and can be rinsed and reused frequently.

## Eazy plug substrate

An easy-to-use, stable, and clean substrate material is Eazy plug. It consists of a special blend of organic materials. Eazy plugs are stably bound, do not decompose, but are compostable. They have a very favourable water/air ratio, are equipped with a basic fertilizer, and have a favourable ph value. They are suitable for the most diverse hydroponic systems.

## Peat substrate

Peat is an organic sediment that has grown extremely slowly in bogs. Peat has a high spring and water storage capacity. The latter can lead to condensation when irrigated. Since peat is also very sour, it is only used in mixtures. Coconut and peat pots are often used to grow seeds. Unfortunately, despite fine mesh, impurities in the hydroponic system cannot be completely avoided. However, it is compostable.

## Substrates floating for hydroponics

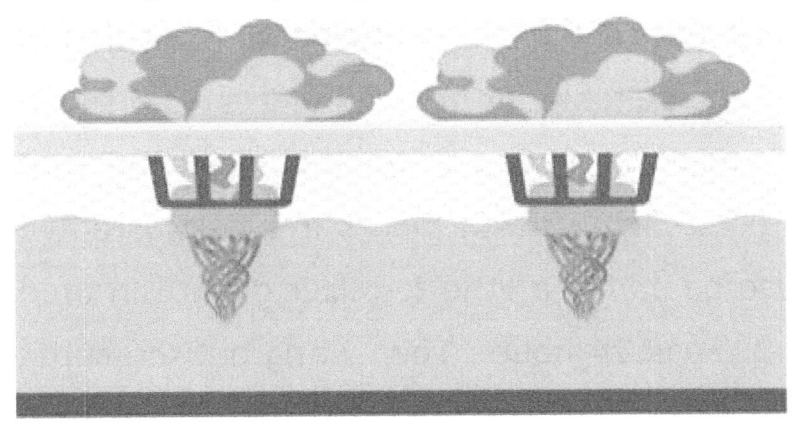

The optimal supply of nutrients and oxygen to roots in hydroponic systems is the main reason for faster and more vigorous plant growth compared to cultivation in soil. In aeroponic cultivation systems, substrates are not used. They are highly efficient but also require optimal monitoring to avoid failures. In most cases, such as nft, low tide, or dwc, work with substrates.

## Hydroponics substrates

There is a selection of inorganic or organic hydroponic substrates with very favorable plant growth properties:

Higher porosity compared to earth

Easily routable so that plants consume little energy Easy access to nutrient solution to the roots

Easy to drain, so that oxygen can penetrate from the air.

## Preparation of substrates

Horticultural rockwool (not to be confused with insulating rockwool, which is treated and suitable for growing plants) is a substrate with a high ph, and it should be lowered. For this, soak the cuttings cubes as well as the 7x7x6.5cm growth blocks in ph-adjusted water at 5.5 to which will also be added a little fertilizer growth in order to arrive at an ecc. of 1.2. Soak 24 hours. Then wring out the cuttings slightly without breaking them. They are ready for use.

As for the clay balls, rinse thoroughly until there is no more liquid brick red color flowing. The clay balls are a substrate with an underlying tendency (high ph), which will cause a regular ph rise in the first weeks of use. Then, the ph should become more stable, as the beads take the ph of the nutrient solution that passes through them.

## Germination and transplantation

Once your ldr has been prepared, take the cuttings cubes. A hole is already present in the center of the cube, the one used to introduce a cutting. Being too deep to germinate a seed, it is advisable to take a small wad on the corner of the cube to fill the bottom of the hole (one can also make another hole less deep). It also is advisable to soak them for 24 hours in lukewarm water to promote seed germination. Once the seed is in place, cover the hole with some rockwool (without packing it, to avoid passing the light). Place your cubes preferably under a mini-greenhouse, and this will prevent the cube of ldr from drying out too quickly, the mini-greenhouse keeping an ambient humidity of about 80%. As soon as the young shoot is well-formed, you can start irrigating it with a little fertilizer (usually ½ of the growth dosage). At this stage, the cubes are irrigated manually. It is advisable to fill the bottom of the mini-greenhouse with clay ball so that the bottom of the ldr cubes do not come into direct contact with the solution poured through the cubes. Regularly check the stage of development of the roots. As soon as the roots have passed through the cuttings cube, place the cube in the 7x7 cube, then put the seedlings back into the mini-greenhouse. Once the roots are out of the cube 7x7cm, bury the cube in the clay ball and so that a corner of the cube is below one of the drippers (the nutrient solution will spread itself in all the cube).

If you have used neon lights (recommended for young shoots and cuttings) during the first 2 weeks of growth, consider positioning your high-pressure lamp at least 1m from the top of the young shoots in order not to burn them. Gradually lower the lamp from day to day up to 40 cm from the top of plants if you use a 400w (30cm for a 250w).

Then keep this distance throughout the growth and flowering phase.

**JAMIE BACKYARD**

# Chapter 4:
# Lightning

Plant growth is influenced by many factors that influence each other, such as soil composition, nutrients, soil and humidity, temperature, and light. Light is the most important growth factor for most plants. If one does not have bright, cool stands on which robust and less heat-requiring plants can hibernate, then only with the help of artificial light sources the seasonal lack of natural sunlight can be counteracted.

Light is the visible part of the electromagnetic radiation to the human eye. With the help of light, the plants can carry out and maintain vital photosynthesis (carbon dioxide assimilation). The illuminance (number "lux" per m2 of plant surface) plays a decisive role here, also called light intensity. An important product of carbon dioxide assimilation is the oxygen that is important to us. Photosynthesis is mainly influenced by the violet-blue and orange-red spectrum of the light, which should be taken into account when choosing the light sources (lamps).

Most plants absorb light over their green leaves. The light gives them energy. With this energy, the plants produce sugar and starch. This is food that the plants need to grow. So, they could not grow without light. Plants suck water and nutrients out of the earth. They take a gas over the air. It's called carbon dioxide. These substances convert the plants into sugar and starch. For this, they need the power of light. Incidentally, the transformation is called photosynthesis. Plants release oxygen into the air.

This is a gas that humans and animals need to breathe. Where many plants grow, the air is always good. In forests, for example, there is a lot of oxygen. Too little light leads to the so-called geilwuchs, whereby root development and leaf growth are neglected in favor of the growth of length so that the plant can get better at a light source. This makes sense when other larger plants cover the smaller one. However, if there is too little light at all, for example, in the interior, the plant can logically still be so long and will not get a photon. Also, one can observe in plant growth that they always stretch to the sun. The shadow side of a plant grows faster and faster, so that it inclines towards the sun, to get a maximum of radiation.

But not only the direction, but also the nature of the light changes the growth of the plant. Depending on the intensity and wavelengths, different substances form, or the plant generally grows more or less well. In order to ensure this environmental factor, one can use artificial light in the form of led plant light, which covers all the wavelengths required for growth and promise better results than purely monochrome light.

## Photosynthesis

Photosynthesis is the biochemical reaction that makes life on earth possible for us. Photosynthesis involves plants and certain bacteria to use light, water, and carbon dioxide to put something new out of them: glucose and oxygen. From low energy inorganic substances with the help of solar energy high- energy organic substances. Chemically speaking, the following molecular formula describes photosynthesis:

$6CO_2 + 6H_2O + \text{light energy} \rightarrow C_6H_{12}O_6 + 6O_2$

Here it can be seen that water ($H_2O$) and carbon dioxide ($CO_2$) is required so that the chemical process of reduction can produce sugars or carbohydrates ($C_6H_{12}O_6$) and oxygen ($O_2$). In detail, the process of photosynthesis is very complex and consists of several interdependent processes. Important: photosynthesis is called a redox reaction, i.e., a reduction-oxidation reaction. But where exactly does photosynthesis take place? The green plants have their color through the green leaf pigment, the chlorophyll. Chlorophyll is found in the membranes of chloroplasts, the organelles in the cells of plants. Very important: the chlorophyll can absorb sunlight, which is needed for the process. In the chloroplasts, which are only a few micrometres in size, the entire photosynthesis takes place. In a single cell, there are sometimes many hundreds of chloroplasts.

In general, photosynthesis can be subdivided into two processes that are inseparable for their success: the light reaction (primary or photoreaction) - here, chemical energy is provided - and the dark reaction (secondary or synthesis reaction), the uses chemical energy from the light reaction to synthesize the high-energy substances.

For us as humans, the most important thing about photosynthesis is that it produces a "waste product", the oxygen vital for us and other living beings. At the same time, the poisonous co2 for us is reduced, because it is consumed.

## How photosynthesis works

The plant transports the water required for photosynthesis (h2o) into the chloroplasts of the leaves. There, the photosynthesis also runs off. At the bottom of the sheet, there are guard cells. These coordinate the exchange of gases: carbon dioxide (co2) flows from the outside into the intercellular spaces. After the photosynthesis, the oxygen (o2) is released via these guard cells.

For photosynthesis, the plant needs light in addition to carbon dioxide and water. The absorption of sunlight is the responsibility of chlorophyll. Chlorophyll is the green dye in the leaves. Carbon dioxide, water, and light convert the plant into oxygen and glucose (c6 h12 o6). The formula for photosynthesis is 6h2o + 6 co2 + light = 6 o2 + c6 h12 o6. Translated, the formula means that the plant needs 6 hydrogen molecules, 6 carbon dioxide molecules, and light to make 6 oxygen molecules and glucose.

The glucose is converted into starch by the plant and is needed by it to carry out the synthesis of fats and proteins, i.e., the food of the plants. The conversion of glucose into starch has one important reason: glucose is a monosaccharide, a simple sugar. In contrast, starch is a polysaccharide.

As a polysaccharide, starch is hardly soluble. This has the advantage that the starch remains in the plant even with heavy water loss. The most important thing about photosynthesis for us humans is the absorption of carbon dioxide and the release of the vital oxygen for us.

## Effects of artificial light on plant

The effect of artificial light on plant growth depends on the artificial light to which the plant is exposed. Some light can offer growth benefits to plants, supporting them in environments with little sunlight.

Others can inhibit the growth process and ultimately kill them. Artificial light differs considerably from the amount of usable light generated for plants. Growers must examine every light source before exposing a plant to it in the long run.

## Effects on growth

Artificial light is not designed for plant growth and only produces a small amount of light compared to the sun. As a result, plants need to work harder to derive the same nutritional effect from artificial light.

According to garden guides, this can lead to odd growth patterns in plants when plants stem toward the light source to support photosynthesis. Plants can develop long spindly branches and browning leaves.

## Heat burns

Artificial light that produces light through heat, such as infrared and incandescent lighting sources can burn plants exposed to them for too long.

Only a small percentage of light produced is usable by the plant. The rest is mainly heat, which only serves to dry out the plant and inhibit growth. Limit periods that plants have been exposed to these types of light sources too early in the growth cycle.

## Fluorescent advantage

Fluorescent lamp sources can serve as a much more efficient means of light for indoor plants. Only 13 to 20 percent of fluorescent light is produced with heat, according to the green pages of the Montreal botanical garden. Growers can combine different fluorescent lamps during the day to best mimic sunlight. They avoid making plants work too hard for nutrients and can increase overall plant health. Fluorescent light also provides a stopgap for outside plants that need to be brought in during the winter months.

Incandescent lamps are thermal radiators and emit most of the absorbed energy in the form of heat, and they are the most unsuitable lamp type for additional exposure. The spectrum of light is mainly located in the orange-red area so that it can lead to hazing of the plants, although intense exposure to incandescent light since the blue-violet portion of the spectrum is completely absent. Reflector lamps, deco, and halogen lamps hardly change this. It is urgently necessary to warn against using so-called plant lamps with incandescent lamps in the winter for additional exposure because the colored glass bulbs do not change their deficient properties for plant exposure. With halogen spotlights, however, individual plants can be effectively lighted out of the vessel. With lamps around 50 watts of power consumption, optimal illumination is often given. The normal room lighting in winter is not sufficient for assimilatory plant exposure. Although incandescent lamps have the lowest acquisition costs of all lamp types, they are the most uneconomical sources of energy in terms of energy. For this reason, the European Union decided to end incandescent lamps by 2012; from 1 September 2009, the 100- watt lamp was already excluded from sale. For the plants, therefore, the "replacement" by energy-saving lamps is a plant physiological "benefit", because the radiation spectrum of energy-saving lamps (esl) unwanted route growth is permanently prevented, as well as by the high-pressure discharge lamp.

Fluorescent lamps (low-pressure discharge lamps) they are popularly referred to as fluorescent or neon tubes, the lighting technician calls them low-pressure gas discharge lamps.

Under the name "three-band fluorescent lamps", the lamp industry offers an excellent light source with very good light colors, which bring an excellent light output of up to 95 lumens per watt of power consumption. By reducing the lamp diameter to 26 mm, only about 10% energy savings can be recorded. Even more effective are the t 5 lamp types with only 16 mm diameter, which come to a lumen output of over 105, but can only be operated with electronic ballast (ecc).

The industry has also come up with something to the fluorescent lamps; outstanding is the complete set's (lamp + light, including plug and cable) to consumer-friendly prices, which may be partially installed in mounting walls. The cost of the lamps alone, which can be screwed into almost any existing lamp due to the reduced diameter (the distance of the pins has remained), are about 24$, the complete set's at about 60 to 180$ for field lamps.

Some compact fluorescent lamps have an incandescent screw base (e14/e27) so that this lamp type can be screwed into almost any incandescent lamp. Other compact lamps require an adapter integrated into the luminaire with suitable equipment (starter, capacitor, ballast) for the socket. The industry indicates that a compact fluorescent lamp with 20 watts of power consumes the same amount of light as an incandescent light bulb of 100 watts, but with a much better spectrum for photosynthesis and a useful burn time of 6,000- 12,000 hours. In a correspondingly good reflector lamp, a small round vessel can be illuminated optimally. Fluorescent lamps. Have with the commercially available light colors for plants, but also aquariums and terrariums, optimal spectrum, and a sufficient orange-red and blue-violet ray portion; the 3-band lamps also have an optimum in the green area that is important for humans. With the help of aesthetic screens, roller blinds, etc. A glare-free suspension can be made possible towards the room.

The suspension height should be 50 - 80 cm above the leaf surface; with cactuses and succulents, you can approach the tops of plants up to 20 cm, which improves the light yield for the "light-hungry" plant species. Fluorescent lamps attract dust, so they need to be dusted from time to time. High-pressure vapor discharge lamps.

Mercury high - pressure lamps with output ranges of 50, 80 and 125 watts are being used in homes and hobby areas, as well as in aquariums and terrariums, due to the ever better and more attractive luminaires. They sit so deep in the lights with special reflectors that the perfectly suitable assimilatory light is emitted glare-free.

However, if the living room atmosphere is adversely affected (in very large plants), as described in the introduction, exposure during the night can be done. The lamps have the optimal blue-violet spectrum and low red light content; they should be suspended 50 to 150 cm above the leaf surface depending on the power consumption and plant species (pendant luminaires) or installed on the wall (wall luminaires). The efficiency is about four times as high as incandescent, with a much better composition of the light radiation for the plant. High-pressure mercury lamps must be operated with a ballast that is installed either in the luminaire dome or externally. Due to cable construction, the lights can be suspended in a height variable. After about 3 minutes, the full light output is reached; a reignition is possible only after cooling the lamp. As special lamps are required for this type of lamp, with vde and gs symbols, the industry increasingly offers excellent luminaires on the market. These complete sets cost about 140 to 300$, depending on the design and material of the lamp. The aim is light with a warm white color (e.g., hql - super deluxe, hpl - comfort); the complete sets usually have a plug-in connection or can be latched in busbars with the corresponding additional plug. High-pressure mercury lamps with a power consumption of more than 125 watts can be used in very large flower windows, orangeries, and hobby greenhouses, as larger areas can be illuminated here with greater distance; the luminaires must be approved for damp and wet rooms (vde 0100).

Metal halide vapor high-pressure lamps are a further development of high- pressure mercury lamps. These lamps are used in corresponding fixtures in the hobby greenhouse, as well as in large "real" flower windows and conservatories. Again, it is advisable to acquire the lamp and the lamp ready to plug in the complete set, with prices starting from $ 150 upwards; among other things, compact lamps with a power of 35 - 70 and 150 watts are used. In the living area, the warm white light color (wol) is preferred.

The ballast and ignitor are placed externally or integrated into the luminaire. Due to their high performance, these lamps are also suitable for higher suspension or longer distances. Sodium vapor high-pressure lamps. Only the special lamps with the color rendering level 1b/2a, which are also suitable for display and accent lighting, are used for the assimilatory exposure in the indoor greenery. These improved high - pressure sodium lamps, some of which are filled with xenon and halides, are also well suited for assimilation in residential, hobby, office, and exhibition rooms/foyers; they are operated in open luminaires because only negligible UV radiation is emitted. To operate the lamps (35-

100 w) ballast and ignitor are necessary; electronic equipment offers other advantages (energy saving, light color stability, etc.). Led = light emitting diodes (examples can be found under led - plant light). They are the star of the "lighting sky" because they emit light with very low electrical power consumption with almost no loss. Currently,

they achieve 65 lumens per watt. The wavelength range in which they emit radiation as light is between 400 and 700 nanometers (nm). However, in order to get the same light output (light intensity) as with fluorescent and high-pressure discharge lamps, hundreds of diodes would have to be used, which would be very expensive at the moment. It must also be clarified by plant-building experiments, how much energy is released in the different wavelength ranges, and how the absence of radiation below 400 nm affects the growth in length.

## What is a led?

A light-emitting diode (also luminescence diode, short led for light-emitting diode or light-emitting diode) is an electronic semiconductor device.

If current flows through the diode in the forward direction, it emits light, infrared radiation, or even ultraviolet radiation with a wavelength-dependent on the semiconductor material. Conventional light bulbs convert the electricity into heat first. That's why you lose a lot of energy, about 95%. Light-emitting diodes, in contrast to light bulbs and glow plugs, convert the current directly into light. Therefore, led luminaires consume only a fraction of the stoma that would be needed for lighting with conventional lamps. Nevertheless, the brightness of the led bulbs compared to traditional light bulbs, which usually consume 10 times as much electricity as costs, comparable, and sometimes better.

The direct conversion of the current into light causes little unused waste heat and thus increases the efficiency. Overall, led lamps offer significantly more light with less power consumption!

Led lamps differ from energy-saving lamps in that they do not contain toxic metals such as mercury. For this reason, energy-saving lamps must not be disposed of as normal household waste but must be disposed of as hazardous waste. When an energy-saving lamp breaks down, it can cause a health risk to humans and pets.

Similar to energy-saving lamps, led lamps consume up to 85 percent less energy than conventional incandescent lamps. Thus, they contribute to the reduction of co2 emissions. Probably the most important advantage is their longevity of up to 25,000 hours. Their ideal use can be found in areas where light is switched on for a long time. Unfortunately, led bulbs are not cheap. A high-quality led lamp costs, on average, between 20 and 40 euros. But most dealers give up to 5 years warranty. With led lamps, you can save a lot of energy costs. They are a sustainable alternative to conventional light bulbs and a serious substitute for energy- saving lamps. Who hesitates, can hope that the purchase price of led lamps in the coming years decline.

**What does the led offer?**
- General lighting in industry and household
- Mobile applications such as led pocket lamps

- Robust and low-maintenance street lighting
- Low -maintenance traffic lights and emergency lighting
- Robust automotive lighting systems
- New products with high integration density (mobile phone flash, led beamer)
- Innovative products for light therapy and plant lighting.

## Advantages of led

- Lifetime with 50,000 hours is about 20 times longer than with bulbs - saving even when the bulbs are replaced
- High efficiency and low energy consumption
- Low heat development
- No release of UV rays Shock and vibration resistant
- Little glare
- No humming noises
- Great variety of types
- All rgb colors are possible.

# Chapter 5:
# Guide To Create Your Own Hydroponic System

For a hydroponics system, build yourself a simple "dwc - deep water cultivation system". It sounds complicated, but it is not. All that is needed are as follows:

- Waterproof plastic box with lid size approx. 50 x 40cm, height approx. 15 cm (from the hardware store or whatever else is around)
- Net pots
- Matching hole drill for mesh pots Aquarium pump with ventilation stone Timer
- Planting substrate, z. Clay balls
- Water
- Hydroponics fertilizers
- Ph test strips for ph determination
- An ec meter for measuring the conductivity, i.e., the fertilizer content of the water
- If an indoor operation is planned, possibly a plant lamp Aeration stone in "dwc" nutrient container.

## Guide to hydroponics in deep water cultivation - dwc

Drill 4 to 6 holes in the removable lid, depending on the size of the box. The holes must be so large that the used network pots find space but cannot slip through. That's it.

To make the box with the lid and the network pots from a passive system to an active system, you get yourself an aquarium air pump with aeration stone (internet about 20 euros). If you want to operate the box indoors, please make sure that the pump is as quiet as possible.

The aerator stone is placed as an oxygen supplier in the box. The best way to control the air pump is by using a timer. By the way, dwc is a very effective, simple system, with which you can familiarize yourself very well with hydroponics and simply try different things.

Now you just have to put the prepared plants in the nets and put the nets in the holes of the box.

Fill water up to approx. 1 cm above the lower edge of the mesh pots and add hydroponic fertilizer according to the manufacturer's instructions.

Turn on the pump via the timer every 30 minutes for about 15 minutes - so the roots are supplied with oxygen. Caution: only hold in the box filled with water, when all electrical consumers have been disconnected.

## Hydroponics for beginners

Look for a container or impervious tank.

Paint with a translucent black spray and allow it to dry. Measure the width and length of your container with a tape measure and use them to cut a styrofoam panel a little smaller than the container, so it can easily adapt to changing water levels. When you have cut the styrofoam, make holes to place the pots you are going to grow. The amount will depend on big is the polystyrene container.

Then place a pump powerful enough to provide your plants with the necessary oxygen. You can ask for advice on this in specialized hydroponics stores.

Connect an airline to the pump. This must be long enough to reach the bottom of the tank or, at least, float in the center of the vessel so that the resulting oxygen bubbles reach the plant roots properly.

Install the hydroponic system. To achieve this, you must fill the tank with a nutrient solution, place the polystyrene plate with the plants inside, fill it with pots, then plug in and start the pump to start growing them.

Preparing your hydroponic garden at home is ideal for planting lettuce, tomatoes, peppers, celery, or cucumbers, plants perfect for aquatic culture. The soil will act as a means of reserving nutrients essential for plant growth.

## Benefits of home-grown hydroponics

The hydroponic system is a simple, clean, and productive culture technique. Among its advantages, it should be noted that it can be applied to any field and for almost all products and that, in addition, it does not require large amounts of water to achieve it. Of course, to obtain good results of culture, it is necessary to keep an exhaustive control of the needs of the plant and the nutritional solutions which you will bring them to ensure optimal growth. To find out more about the hydroponic system, do not hesitate to consult the specialized stores. They will give you the keys so that you can properly build a homemade hydroponic garden.

# Chapter 6:
# Plant Nutrition

Before water becomes a nutrient solution, it must first be said that water is not equal to water. Water is very different in its composition. The division of hard and soft water calls already in the budget consideration. When washing dishes, washing clothes, and cooking care must be taken. And just when casting the house plants, the use of the existing "irrigation water" must be considered. With which water hardness the water flows out of the pipe, you will find out at your waterworks. Mostly for watering (of plants in soil), softened (soft) water is recommended. The use of collected rainwater is recommended today only after filtering with activated carbon. But who runs this effort?

Up to water hardness of approx. 8°dh (German hardness), you can fertilize with normal hydroponic liquid fertilizer or in powder form for dissolving (Flory 9). These special fertilizers are specially made for hydroponics. They can also be used for plants in soil. Conversely, you should not use "normal" flower fertilizers for hydroponics.

So, fertilization is the replacement of nutrients that the plants have removed from the soil or nutrient solution with the help of their roots. With "fertilizer", we also commonly refer to the nutrients for the plants. These are construction and supplies for the plant. They are taken up via the leaves and over the roots and transformed into the leaf-green with the help of sunlight into the body's substances (assimilates). The most important nutrient is carbon. It is taken as carbon dioxide in the air and passes through the stomata of the leaf underside into the leaf green (chlorophyll). We only influence the uptake of carbon dioxide from the air insofar as we have to ensure sufficient air movement in the leaf area because the proportion of carbon dioxide in the air is only about 0.03% and is therefore quickly consumed. The air movement allows the supply of constantly new carbon dioxide to the leaf. In greenhouses of commercial horticulture, this is achieved by the so-called $CO^2$ degassing and (at least in the summer) by artificial air circulation or air supply with the help of strong fans. Indoor plants manage with the lower supply of carbon dioxide by the movement of air in the room. And yet it may be advantageous to the room air movement by increased ventilation (no drafts) or by a small and slow-running fan, especially in the warm season to promote. This is especially important in a plant showcase or when dense curtains on the window make it difficult to recirculate the air. Outside plants usually come out with the carbon dioxide, because there is always a weak air movement there.

Fertilization by the supply of nutrients through the roots, on the other hand, is subject to our influence. We have the power to give the plant the nutrients it needs to grow and thrive.

For decades, manufacturers have been making it easy for us to provide the plant with nutrients. The fertilizers are composed according to the requirements of the crop. Fertilizers of different compositions make it possible to adapt fertilization to different needs. There is a fundamental difference between fertilizer for soil culture and hydroponic culture in that plants in the soil are supplied with organic fertilizer (such as manure and manure). However, inorganic fertilizers can be used as well. On the other hand, earth less plants need a fertilizer that does not require the soil to be prepared for planting, but that is directly receptive to the roots. The most obvious difference is the nutrient nitrogen (n = nitrogen). These can take the plants in the amide form, i.e., uric acid. Earth less plants cannot do that. If one were to add fertilizer to the nutrient solution, the nitrogen of which contains too much urea, there would inevitably be a "tipping over" of the nutrient solution.

There is one more important difference: the fertilizer content of the nutrient solution for hydroponics never flows into the soil and therefore, cannot pollute it unless, in the rain, the hydroponic tank overflows without the overflowing nutrient solution or the fertilizer containing water for the purpose of collecting later use. In contrast, the fertilized soil solution in soil plants flows deep and wide into the soil layers outside after a downpour and can lead to pollution of the groundwater, the later drinking water. Waste soil solution is lost to the plant supply.

In hydroponic culture, no nutrient solution is usually lost unused. Therefore, the water consumption in hydroponic culture is much lower than in the soil culture.

As fertilizer for the hydroponic culture, three different forms are used: nutrient salt, liquid fertilizer, or ion exchange fertilizer. Then it is subdivided according to the composition: nitrogen-stressed, phosphorous-retained, potassium-reinforced, etc., depending on the use of plants with special needs. The (normal) regulating fertilizer is slightly potassium-enriched and meets the needs of most ornamental and indoor plants. There are also fertilizers that contain only one nutrient or two or three nutrients. It is used when, for a short time or during a particularly needy growth phase (flowering), this single nutrient is needed to an increased extent.

The composition of a (normal) fertilizer is characterized by the three (or four) characters npk. N is nitrogen (nitrogen), p is phosphorus, k is potassium. Often one finds on the label also the fourth sign mg, and it stands for magnesium. These characters are followed by numbers separated by a hyphen or colon. Example: npkmg 123162 or 12: 3: 16: 2. It is the composition, in this case, a potassium-stressed fertilizer, which is mostly used for hydroponics. There are other compositions as well. Thus, in the hydroponic commercial horticulture in the first growth phase, a nitrogen-stressed fertilizer is often used in the bloom phase, a phosphorus-rich, and in the fruit phase a potassium accentuated.

Cacti usually need a specially-made fertilizer, namely a more potassium-stressed (because of the strong water binding of the tissue). Another fertilizer contains little or no nitrogen. It is added to the nutrient solution only when the desired ph value has been determined. Namely, it can be influenced by selecting a particular nitrogen fertilizer type of ph.

The addition of ammonium allows the lowering of the ph value, which, however, requires experience. A disadvantage is (can be) the use of liquid hydroponic fertilizer and dissolved hydroponic fertilizer, as this shortened the cleaning interval of the vessels.

By evaporation of a part of the water of the nutrient solution, especially if the plants have beneficial warm feet. Part of the fertilizer crystallizes out and settles in expanded clay. This should be rinsed with every renewal of the nutrient solution. Here's a word about so-called fertilizer.

There is no artificial fertilizer! This is just the expression of people who lack understanding of manure and fertilizer. One should also speak better of mineral fertilizer.

The nutrient solution consists of water to which all nutrients necessary for plant growth are added. This sounds easier than it is. At this point, therefore, only the necessary is to be conveyed. Anyone who wants to know exactly can acquire all deepening knowledge under advanced hydroponics.

## Irrigation water

Proper fertilization depends on the particular water quality in each case. Depending on their location or origin, irrigation water may contain varying amounts of both beneficial and undesirable substances (ions). There is, therefore, no patent remedy for the fertilization of "hydroponics" incidentally, this also applies to all other culture processes, including those inorganic substrates. Simplified, the different waters can be divided into the following classes:

- Low salt with low conductivity and low hardness, including rainwater
- Medium salt content and medium hardness
- High salt content and high hardness
- The water supply companies provide detailed information on tap water quality, either directly or via the internet. Beware of in-house water softening systems. These change the composition of the tap water considerably. Softened water is unsuitable as water for plants.

## Fertilizers

Even if fertilizer is so declared, there is no special fertilizer for "hydroponics" it depends rather on the respective water quality, which fertilizer is suitable. There are the following options for the fertilization of hydroponics:

- Ion exchanger

- Liquid fertilizer
- Salt fertilizers

In principle, do not use organic fertilizers, as microbial decomposition of the contained organic matter can lead to a sustained lack of oxygen in the accumulation zone and fungal growth on the substrate surface.

**JAMIE BACKYARD**

# Conclusion

We've come a long way throughout the course of this book. Starting with a definition of hydroponics, we're covered a lot of information that will help you to get started on your own hydroponic garden. Before we close, let's go over a brief summary of what we covered and share some words on where to go from here.

Hydroponics has been around for literally ages but it is only just starting to pick up some serious interest. These gardens can take a bit of work to set up and maintain but they offer a great way of growing crops.

We focused here on those looking to get started with hydroponics, so we tailored our information towards the beginner. The lessons we covered, however, have everything the beginner needs to get started and begin the road to expert.

We have six primary setups to choose from when it comes to what kind of system we want to set up. We saw how to set up deep water, wicking and drip systems. These are the easiest systems for DIY setups and beginners but there are also aeroponics, ebb and flow and nutrient film technique systems.

These systems are more complicated than is recommended for a beginner one, but I encourage you to research these more as you get more comfortable with hydroponics.

There are four key elements that we looked at as the operation cycle of the hydroponic garden. These are soiling, seeding, lighting and trimming. By understanding how each of these elements works, we are able to handle the growing cycle of our plants. There are many options available for soiling and several for lighting. Finding the combination that is right for you will take some research but it should ultimately be decided on what plants you want to grow.

Speaking of plants, we have seen that there are a ton of plants that work really well in hydroponic gardens. Herbs grown in a hydroponic garden have 30% more aromatic oils than those grown in soil. Lettuce in particular absolutely adores growing hydroponically. Each plant has its own preferences when it comes to how much water it wants, the pH level it likes best and the temperature that it needs to grow. For this reason, we have to research our plants and make sure that we only grow those that are compatible together.

We also learned how to mix our own nutrient solutions so that we can provide our plants with what they need to grow. There are a lot of pre-mixed options available for purchase as well.

Taking control of our own mix is just another way we are able to get closer to our plants and provide for them to the best of our ability.

The importance of maintaining a clean garden cannot be stressed enough and so we spent time learning how we care for our gardens. To do this, look at how often each step of maintenance needs to be performed and plan ahead so that you don't forget. It's super important that we take care of our plants because we don't want them in dirty environments nor do we want them to be overly stressed. A dirty environment and a stressed plant are a recipe for infestation and infection. We explored some of the most common pests that attack our plants. However, we didn't cover all of them. That would take a whole book. The pests we covered are the most likely ones you will have to deal with but that doesn't mean they will be the only ones. It is a good thing we also learned how to prevent pests. The preventive steps we learned will also help us to spot any pests we did not cover. If you find something you don't recognize in one of your traps then you know it's time for more research. Remember too that not every insect is a pest, some help us out by eating pests!

Infection is a risk with all gardens and so our number one tool in preventing harmful pathogens from attacking our plants is to make sure that our plants are nice and strong. We clean our gardens, we provide them with nutrients mixed to their liking, we give them the love and care they need and in doing this we keep them healthy and unstressed. While infection can still take hold in a healthy plant, it is far more likely to attack stressed plants.

Finally, we looked at mistakes that are common to beginning hydroponic gardeners. We also exploded those myths that surround hydroponics to dispel the lies and untruths surrounding our newfound hobby. Searching online for tips or mistakes will reveal many discussions with hydroponic gardeners that are written specifically to help beginners like you to have the easiest, most enjoyable time possible getting into this form of gardening. If you're excited to get started then I suggest you begin planning out your garden now. You will need to dedicate a space for it and pick which system is most appealing to you and your skill level. Write down the plants you are most interested in growing and begin gathering information about them; what environment do they like best? What temperature? How much light do they need? What pH level?

Once you know what plants you want to grow and what system you want, you can start to build a shopping list. Along with the hardware to set up the system itself, don't forget to get some pH testing kits and an EC meter.

Also make sure you have cleaning material, as you know now how important it is to sanitize and sterilize your equipment. This is also a great time to build your maintenance schedule.

Once you have this information you can return to this book and use it as a manual for walking through every step of the growing process.

The information that we covered will take you from beginner and, along with the application of practice, turn you into a pro in no time. But most importantly, don't forget to have fun!

Made in the USA
Las Vegas, NV
24 August 2022